LITTLE CRAZY CHILDREN
ARE JANGLING THE KEYS
OF THE KINGDOM

RICHARD P. SINAY

LITTLE CRAZY CHILDREN ARE JANGLING THE KEYS OF THE KINGDOM

THE ESTRANGEMENT EPIDEMIC IN AMERICA

PALMETTO
PUBLISHING
Charleston, SC
www.PalmettoPublishing.com

Little Crazy Children Are Jangling the Keys of the Kingdom:
Copyright © 2024 by Richard P. Sinay

First Edition

Hardcover ISBN: 979-8-8229-4364-3
Paperback ISBN: 979-8-8229-4365-0
eBook ISBN: 979-8-8229-4366-7

To Tina, who lovingly supported me throughout this writing,
despite her difficult health struggles.

To Claudia, whose insights after reading my rough draft helped
reformulate my book to what it has become.

To Brian and Jennie, both of whom I forgive,
who inadvertently inspired me to write the book.

To All Undeserving Parents who have suffered
the indignity of estrangement.

"Twenty years from now you will be more disappointed by the things that you didn't do than by the ones you did do. So throw off the bowlines. Sail away from the safe harbor. Catch the trade winds in your sails. Explore. Dream. Discover."

Mark Twain

Table of Contents

Part III: Written In Defense of Our Parenting and My Grandparenting

Preface

"How sharper than a serpent's tooth it is
to have a thankless child!"

William Shakespeare, *King Lear*

wrote this book for two different but related audiences: all the parents who have suffered the indignity of estrangement, and to those who imposed that affliction on their family members. For the estranged, I wanted to express how it feels to be abandoned by one's children. I wanted to capture the emotional pain associated with such a treatment, hoping those who have suffered the same fate would identify with the pain. I also wanted to share with them the knowledge that I gained that helped me deal with the problem of being estranged. At the same time, I also wanted to show to those who are doing the estranging what the impacts of such an action are. Estrangers are those who do the estranging and their choice to do so has a greater impact on the people they are estranging than perhaps they realize. I want to communicate what that impact is like. Also, although I am not an expert in psychology nor am I a psychologist, I offer some suggestions for the estranged person's problems. I will offer what I learned from my experience, and from my reading what the estranged can do to handle this problem more effectively. For professional help, I suggest a therapist who knows about estrangement.

I also wanted to show what the experts have been saying about the generations who think tossing parents and grandparents under the bus is not a problem. The reader will discover that parents who are considered by any standard to be good and even great parents are being estranged. This is not normal and I want to make as many estranged readers aware of the problem of estrangement to learn why that is. I will also discuss the standard reasons for estrangement that happen in every generation. There are justifiable reasons for a child to estrange a parent, and there are those that are not justifiable.

I wanted to expose the paradigm shift in American Society family values that indicates younger people do not value or respect the elderly or their older parents. Even though I cannot indict all members of these generations, the significance of the number who have estranged a member of their family has been determined to be epidemic in proportion. The statistics show that this is not a fluke and that this estrangement of parents and grandparents is happening at significant levels. The current level of estrangement has been described as a social phenomenon that signals a deterioration of family unity in our society.

Because of the sheer embarrassment of being estranged from one's children and grandchildren, it is difficult to discuss anything of this nature with people that one even knows well. No one wants their friends to know that they are estranged from their children and grandchildren. So, the number of people suffering this fate may be more significant than reported. This is not an easy book to write because it will be out there publicly, and many of those I know will discover that I am going through such a difficult situation. Writing the book has helped me to understand the situation better, although it has not helped me solve it. It was not my decision not to solve this family crisis, so I decided to write about how it feels to be a parent without children and grandchildren.

I want to show that it is understood that parents are estranged for egregious behaviors. It needs to be understood that adult children should be able to reject a parent who has been abusive in any way. It is the choice of the adult child to separate from any continued reminder of that misconduct on the part of the parent. However, this is about being estranged for what I believe are unjustified reasons. It is my view, but it is important to realize that parents all over the country are being estranged for unjustified reasons.

I want the reader to learn about the conclusions I have drawn about those who estrange a parent. I want to share the story of those who are unwilling to give a reason for estranging a parent and about those who are unwilling to accept apologies for the mistakes of the parent. I want those suffering from the same problem to recognize that there are forces more significant than one's parenting bringing about this estrangement epidemic. It is essential to understand why this is happening in our society.

Dr. Joshua Coleman was the psychologist I chose to follow because he did go through estrangement with his daughter from his first marriage. Hence, he has unique insights into the experience that most psychologists do not bring. With the help and understanding of Dr. Josh Coleman, the renowned psychologist on this subject, it came to my attention that parents are not entirely responsible for this social phenomenon of estrangement. Instead, it must be laid at the door of a lot of different factors including one particular generation. I know they will not be happy to hear that, but statistical evidence shows it is true. There are significant members of one generation who have chosen to estrange a parent or parents. It has become a hot topic for psychologists around this country and in England. Most of Europe is not affected by this phenomenon, There are several critics of one generation for this cavalier treatment of their parents. Not all members of this generation are doing this, of course, but significant numbers of them are, and it has been deemed an epidemic. Dr. Coleman is not alone in his criticism of those individuals who so cavalierly mistreat their parents and grandparents simultaneously.

I genuinely hope that those parents who have suffered through this problem will find that they are not alone and that millions of people are suffering through this problem. I have written this for the estrangers who perpetrate this folly on their unsuspecting parents and grandparents. I have written it to those who are affected by the estrangement, and as a spokesperson for those estranged. I have written it with the hope that others will find solace in the reading of it and some help in understanding what they are going through. I have written, as Josh Coleman says, "like any writer, I wrote for the solace of getting it out of me and onto the dispassionate, somewhat comforting two-dimensional world of paper and pen" (148). Let's begin.

Introduction

n his book *Rules of Estrangement: Why Adult Children Cut Ties and How to Heal the Conflict*, Dr. Joshua Coleman, renowned estrangement psychologist, states "And that's because today, more than at any other time in our nation's history, children are setting the terms of family life in the United States. If it was once the child's job to earn the parents' love and respect, today it is the parents' job to earn the love and respect of their child and to keep earning these through adulthood" (Coleman 234). In short, the adult children are in charge of their parents. How is this so? Well, it appears that since they became adults, they have decided to exercise their power by telling parents what will or will not happen. Perhaps it is because they did not like being told what to do as children. No one knows the answer to that.

Since I spent so much time reading literature during my career, I cannot help but make a comparison between the Salem Witch Trials and the events going on today with estrangement. This book's title comes from a play by Arthur Miller called *The Crucible*. *The Crucible* is the story of how Salem, Massachusetts, became the only place in America where "witches" were hung (19 of them, to be exact). In the play, the children were sought out to testify against the adults. The children's testimony was accepted, and some two hundred people were arrested and charged with witchcraft. As the town went wild with accusations, the main character of the play, John Proctor, stated that the "little crazy children are jangling the keys of the kingdom" because the children (the girls primarily) who made the accusations were in control of the town. They do and say what they want with impunity; they get away with murder. The witchcraft trials turned the world upside down so that those who used to be powerless were the ones in power; thus, they were "jangling the keys of the kingdom." Dr. Coleman indicated that adults have to earn their children's respect, so the family paradigm has been turned upside down.

In Josh Coleman's book *When Parents Hurt: Compassionate Strategies When You and Your Grown Child Don't Get Along*, he states that "Stanford University psychologist Fred Luskin discovered that finding the impersonal in an event or relationship is critical to our ability to feel insulated from the potential hurt in that event or relationship. His research shows that people who have been deeply hurt often develop a 'grievance story' that causes them to spend a large amount of time reviewing the past, resulting in their feeling victimized and unhappy." (Coleman 44). This book is my own "grievance story" because the actions of my two children have deeply hurt me. I am an estranged father who lost contact with my son and his family four years ago and my daughter within the last year. This writing is an effort to share my story with those estranged parents who have suffered the same fate and to reach out to this community of people who feel equally aggrieved to share what I have discovered in my reading and through my own experience. The purpose is to share how becoming estranged affects the parent or the grandparent and how to deal with it. We have all the books we need from psychologists who tell us what we can do to mend our situations, but few books from the patient's point of view who have suffered this fate.

When my ex-wife told me my son's behavior resulted from genetics, I thought about Joshua Coleman's quote in his book *When Parents Hurt: Compassionate Strategies When You and Your Adult Child Don't Get Along*. In his chapter "Getting It Wrong About Parents," Coleman states: "While some parenting behaviors can create problems in children, I believe we need a much more nuanced and complete picture than the one currently provided by therapists, politicians, and talk show hosts. A larger picture is necessary because influences such as genes, economics, peer groups, siblings, culture, and personality can cause some kids to make their mediocre parents look and feel pretty great. In contrast, others make their exceptional parents look and feel pretty awful. Just by their nature, some children create a lot of parental error and heartache. Some environments create problems in children that have little to do with whether mom and dad are following the latest and greatest parenting advice to a T." (Coleman 9). In other words, a parent is not solely responsible for what happens when estrangement occurs. Other factors contribute to estrangement occurring. The basic behavior of the adult child is a significant contributor to estrangement.

This writing is also part therapy since I have found writing to be an avenue to treat emotional distress. I have often used it in my life to help me understand the actions of others and those of myself. The main gist of this writing is to share with those unfortunate parents that they are NOT responsible for the falling out with their children unless they have committed egregious acts that fostered that estrangement. Those acts include sexual abuse, emotional abuse, alcoholism, excessive gambling, or violence of any nature. I am writing for those parents who did not commit any egregious acts to warrant the estrangement. I am writing to those parents who have been estranged for unjustifiable reasons, although I will discuss those justifiable reasons as well.

Through this writing, I explain how difficult this has been for me as a father who put his children first before anything else. We Baby Boomers were the original "Helicopter" parents who hovered over their child's every move. One friend of my daughter had six different sets of shoes for the activities her parents had arranged for her to participate in. She had dance shoes, soccer shoes, baseball shoes, volleyball shoes, track shoes, and tennis shoes for tennis. She spent her entire time running from one activity to another. Too many of us Baby Boomers gave excessive attention to the children and not enough attention to each other as a couple. This paradigm of parenting was a recipe for a failed marriage. We thought putting the kids on a pedestal was right when it was wrong for a good marriage. We did not know that at the time we raised the kids, and although we both did a great job as parents, our relationship as a couple fell apart. I did not realize this until I read Coleman's comment that stated, "...many parents create a self-fulfilling prophecy by putting all their energy into their children and letting their marriages wither on the vine" (63). Both children were straight-A students throughout their schooling, with one going to the University of California at Santa Barbara and the other to Stanford on a golf scholarship. Getting them to these excellent educational institutions was much work for both parents.

After my estrangement, I suffered emotionally for two years until I got help from Dr. Joshua Coleman. His books and his many articles and seminars for the estranged were extremely beneficial in dealing with the problem. I stopped punishing myself for causing the problem with my son and his family. Dr. Coleman will be quoted throughout the book to help communicate what it is like to be abandoned and give credence to what an expert says about this problem in America.

This book has evolved with time because it is just the nature of writing. Sometimes, writers know what they want to say before they write; other times, writers discover what they want to say as they write. This book has been a process of discovery. This book is primarily written for those good parents who still suffer from losing contact with their adult child despite being an excellent parent. I am one of those parents. Today's social phenomenon of estrangement is affecting many good parents. At the same time, it is essential to remember that there are also good and bad children, even if the environment they grew up in is the same for all the children.

Writing this book will probably end any relationship with my children and grandchildren. Although I am deeply sorry that this has happened, it is out of my control. After many efforts at reconciliation, there appears to be no interest in it. Therefore, I do not write to seek revenge but to understand how something as heinous as this can happen. The book tells the rest of the story. Enjoy the read, even if the subject is revolting.

PART I:

WRITTEN FOR THOSE WHO ESTRANGE THEIR PARENTS, GRANDPARENTS OR SIBLINGS

This book section aims to speak to those estranged from their parents, grandparents, or siblings. It is crucial for those who do such a thing that they understand the ramifications of such an action. Anyone who reads this that has estranged a family member may discover that the impact is far more significant than what they might think. This section will start by identifying the epidemic of estrangement that has flourished in American society.

CHAPTER 1:

The Epidemic of Estrangement in America

I n his highly regarded book *Rules of Estrangement: Why Adult Children Cut Ties and How to Heal the Conflict,* Joshua Coleman states that "No one knows who is going to [be estranged] and who isn't. There are many truly abusive parents whose children would never dream of estranging them; conversely, there are plenty of dedicated parents whose children choose to end the relationship. The fact that so many dedicated parents are estranged today shows that this is part of a larger social phenomenon, more than the problem of any one parent" (Coleman 257). There is a cruel irony to the words of Dr. Coleman. Some parents are abusive to their children, and those children would never think of abandoning their parents. I know of those kinds of families.

On the other hand, there are those parents who raised their children in an idyllic world, and yet they find themselves to be estranged parents. I am one of those. Estrangement is not new to American society, nor any other society, and generation after generation has had this problem. However, estrangement in American society is at an all-time high, and it has become more of a social phenomenon than a run-of-the-mill every-generation estrangement.

Estrangement is what is happening in America in the year 2023. A significant generation is shedding their parents like they are witches. They do so by abandoning, shunning, and ostracizing them. The parents have become strangers (thus, estranged) in their own families. As I indicated, this is happening to more than just parents who made serious mistakes as parents. Estrangement is happening to parents who were good and even outstanding just as Dr. Coleman has indicated. My ex-wife and I were outstanding parents who did our best to raise our two children to be good citizens. In my case, It did not matter to my children that I was an outstanding parent. I have been tossed under the bus for violating their bizarre values for some inexplicable reason. No single expert understands why this is happening at epidemic proportions in America. My ex-wife has not suffered the same fate because she chooses not to challenge their adult behavior. As I write this book, I need to learn about the reason(s) for abandonment. I will address this problem later in the book.

In the past, estrangement was primarily due to parents exercising lousy parenting. Parents who were abusive and committed egregious acts left their children with no choice but to abandon their parent(s). Egregious acts like sexual misconduct, physical abuse, emotional abuse, and other misconduct were the reasons why children decided to become estranged from their parent(s). This is understandable and probably justified behavior on the part of the children. However, we are not talking about becoming estranged from the classic egregious acts on the part of parents. Instead, a different era of estrangement has arrived in American society.

Daniel DeVise comments in a recent article on the internet published by thehill.com, "One-Quarter of Adult Children Estranged from a Parent" is a startling statistic, given that it means one-fourth of eighty million Baby Boomers who are estranged parents. According to the article, this is a "societal shift" from traditional family ties. Also, according to the article, "One recent study, drawing on thousands of interviews with adult children, found that 26 percent reported estrangement from the father. A much smaller 6 percent share had cut ties with mothers."

Although the statistics show a large segment of society touched by estrangement, the numbers are unclear given that people are unwilling to admit that they are estranged from family members. The numbers are more significant than reported, knowing that so many are unwilling to admit to such a failing. There is a great deal of shame associated with being an estranged parent, and so things are kept quiet.

More significantly, Fern Schumer Chapman indicates in another article derived online at psychologytoday.com, "Why So Many Families Are Living With Estrangement," the statistics are appalling:

- "One in four Americans reported being estranged from a relative in a 2019 nationwide survey of 1,340 Americans aged 18 and older. The survey conducted by Karl Pillemer, a professor of human development at Cornell University, showed that more than one-fourth of the respondents—27 percent—reported a current estrangement. Most had a rift with an immediate family member: 24 percent were estranged from a parent, 14 percent from a child, and 30 percent from siblings. The remainder were estranged from other relatives.

- Another study in 2015 also showed that at least 27 percent of Americans are estranged from a member of their own family, and research suggests about 40 percent of Americans have experienced estrangement at some point.

- Estrangement affected one in five families in the United Kingdom, according to a 2015 survey for the British estrangement charity *Stand Alone*. Analysis of 807 members of the *Stand Alone* community who completed a survey showed that 54 percent agreed with the statement that "estrangement or family breakdown is common in our family," and 68 percent of adults estranged from one or more members of their families believe a stigma accompanies family estrangement. The respondents cited the fear of judgment and assumptions of fault or blame as frequent sources of shame."

Many families are affected by estrangement, and although many do not suffer from this problem, there are too many in American society to ignore the issue. Quite a few books written by psychologists attempt to deal with this problem by offering causes and solutions to this crisis. However, there are an equal number of psychologists who are encouraging adult children to cast off their "toxic" parents. It is an industry that is helping to create the problem and, at the same time, offering so-called "solutions" to the estrangement problem. Joshua Coleman has indicated that too many psychologists are using the word "toxic" to describe the parents to the adult children seeking help. Then they suggest that being around "toxic" people is not in the adult child's best interest, and so the estrangement problem got a big boost from the psychologists.

In chapter two, we look at the varying effects of estrangement on the estranged person. Those who estrange a loved one may not realize how damaging it is to the soul of the estranged. Discussing the effects will hopefully elevate one's consciousness about how punishing such a decision is.

CHAPTER 2:

The Effects of Estrangement on the Estranged

The estranger must understand the effects that estrangement has on the estranged. Perhaps estangers, or those doing the estranging, do not know how harsh the impact is on the person or persons they are estranging. This chapter is about the effects of estrangement on estranged parents or grandparents. Many of these effects are incredibly painful for the estranged parent. There is a deep psychological hurt, even to the point of one physically hurting in the head as a result of this action on the part of the adult child. I want to share those effects I experienced so that all readers who have had the same fate may or may not identify with them.

Imagine, first of all, that one does not ever expect to become an estranged person. I not only never thought of such a thing regarding my parents, much less take an action like this. So, when one finds out that one is estranged, many things happen in the head of the estranged. Here are some examples of what happens.

The first effect of estrangement is that it makes the estranged question everything. They begin to question everything they did in the past, thinking they did something wrong and were never told about it. The estranged question all the efforts that were made during their parenthood and wonder what it is that they did wrong. I was told I was a narcissist and that I had been one for many, many years. I cannot imagine my children telling me that when I was so devoted to them, but one of them did. When deemed a "witch," one questions what one did during one's life and how one affected people without knowing it. This is what I mean by the effect of questioning everything one has done in the past. It is troubling and soul-searching. The estranged dwell on this.

Another sad effect of estrangement is that it keeps a person awake for a long time at night. They are wondering what they could have done that deserved such a heinous punishment. I could not sleep peacefully for at least a year or two without thinking about how anyone could be so punitive as to take away my grandchildren. I was always upset and did not know what to do. I had to go into my office and read at night when I could not sleep until I became tired enough to go back to bed and try to fall asleep. This made me tired every day, and falling asleep was difficult.

Another effect on my psyche was that I had bad dreams, and I never had bad dreams before. The dreams predominantly concern my son and his rejection of me. I am always begging him for forgiveness (for what I am not sure) and reconciliation. But he has none to give me and rejects my advances every time. I sometimes dream that my daughter is calling out to me, waking me up. The other night, I screamed out my son's name to come to help me because people were attacking me. I had to wake up to shed the bad dreams. I have never had bad dreams like that, but they happened for almost two years. These dreams about forgiveness were particularly troubling because I discovered that my children have none to give me.

If one does not know what shame feels like, becoming estranged will teach one the hard way. Brene Brown, a famous social scientist, said, "Hey, I was listening to a podcast by a woman who studies shame. Do you know what that word means? I was not sure what it meant. But she said, 'It is that feeling that washes over you, that makes you feel like you are small and not good enough, and that you are not worthy of love and connection with your friends and family.' That is the horrible feeling one has when rejected by a family. It washes over a person like the blood drains from one's body, and one can hardly stand up. This is so true because I have had just such an experience. I experienced shame when I was told for the first time that I was estranged from my son. I retained a lawyer for a car accident I was in with my son in Boulder, Colorado. When she told me I was estranged from my son, the feeling Brene Brown describes came over me just like she described. It was a devastating experience. To be told in that manner was so heartless I nearly collapsed.

Shame also intervenes when it is difficult to discuss with friends how one's kids and grandkids are doing when one does not know. I am ashamed when people ask me how many children and grandchildren I have and where they live. I cannot speak as if I know my children and grandchildren because I do not know what they are doing. I don't even know what their ages are anymore. Shame overwhelms one when one has to reply to someone asking about the grandchildren's ages and other questions. The shame of being estranged by the decision of my children is so punitive that it is hard to describe how punishing it is. Shame is the profound emotion that overwhelms the estranged.

Another dire effect that estrangers perpetrate on the estranged is their isolation from the family during birthdays, holidays, and other significant events in the adult children's and grandchildren's lives. When one cannot celebrate the birthday of one's child or grandchildren, an emptiness eats at the core of one's soul. It is as if they no longer exist and were never a part of me or belong to me in any way. It tears at the soul and beats one down into a helpless state. There is no joy at Christmas anymore, even though I made every effort to make Christmas a special time for my two children when they were growing up. My ex-wife did as well. It is an empty holiday and joyless without them in our lives. It is tough during the Christmas season, but it is also difficult at Thanksgiving, at Easter, during Valentine's Day, and on their birthdays. All these times come and go without a chance to celebrate by talking to them and asking them how they are doing in school. I supported and nurtured my children through twenty-one or two years of their lives and beyond. Despite these efforts, the family has abandoned me. I am left alone without contact with any of my children or grandchildren. My daughter joined my son in her isolation about a year ago, or about three years into my son's rejection. She also has not given me any reason for why she is doing this. As Coleman indicates, "One of the hardest pills to swallow was realizing I meant nothing to people that meant a lot to me" (Coleman 17). Coleman captures, for most people devastated by this behavior, the pain of recognizing that I now meant nothing to them. It is as if the family I helped my entire life disappeared.

Another effect that is so devastating to the estranged parent is the embarrassment (different from shame) of people learning that I am estranged from my children. Whenever someone discusses their kids and grandkids, they ask about my own. I tell them I am estranged from my children and grandchildren. The person questioning me automatically thinks something must be wrong with me to have something like that happen. It is hard to describe how difficult it is to explain how something like that happened. I once explained how my estrangement came about to a couple we knew fairly well and one of them said, "Well, that is your version of the story." The person didn't trust my story even though I told the truth. In other words, people want to know the child's side of the story because they want to hear what heinous things I must have done to deserve such treatment. That is where the embarrassment comes to pass. One feels embarrassed that such a thing is happening in one's life, and people assume it must have been a severe problem that I created alone. One cannot adequately defend oneself. Other people assume that I must have done something seriously wrong. In the judgment of many of my family and friends, I did not.

At the same time, I have had people open up to me and tell me they are suffering the same fate. Because this is a silent epidemic, most people don't go out of their way to discuss their estrangement from their families. I have learned that many people are suffering the fate of estrangement. One finds solace in discovering others are suffering the same problem. Usually, the conversation continues for a while when one meets someone with the same problem. It should be understood that estrangers have put their loved ones in a circle of people going through the same circumstance if only to find comfort and support with the knowledge they are suffering. It is good to find a support group.

Another critical effect of estrangement is the loss of reputation when others learn that we have become estranged from our grandchildren and children. When one is estranged, one's reputation is damaged, and those who learn that one is estranged judge people without knowing the facts. Estrangement is a terrible blow to one's reputation. One's reputation as a father is destroyed by behavior like this. It is a commentary on one's fatherhood, which I thought was as good as possible but certainly not perfect (who is?). I address my parenthood in another part of this book, but when someone is singled out like this, they feel they failed as a parent. Even though I did not fail, becoming estranged makes one feel they have. Estrangers have failed to realize that doing something like this is devastating to a person.

Then there is the feeling of tremendous loss as a parent and as a grandparent. It is the same as if both families had been killed in a horrific car accident. Those families are dead to the estranged and do not exist. It is an excruciating pain that takes a great deal of time to subside but never goes away. It is the same as if they had all been wiped out by a tornado or some such horrific natural accident. But this is no accident. There is just rejection. There is only the pain of loss. It is the loss of the family one once had.

Additionally, the effect of humiliation from being told that one is not worthy of being a part of a family anymore is so hurtful that it is a pain that is indescribable. The pain one feels often drives one to suicidal thoughts with desperate pleas for help. I never entertained a thought like that until I was denied the chance to interact with my grandkids, whom I love enormously. And those thoughts came to my head. Estranging a parent as an action is humiliating.

Then, there is the effect of how powerless one is to do anything about being ostracized. I titled the book "The Kids Are Jangling the Keys of the Kingdom " because the kids have the power, and the estranged have nothing. The children control the kingdom and will tell the estranged what is right and wrong. They have stepped into the parental shoes and decided that what goes is their choice, not the estranged. This is a horrible feeling. I asked my ex-wife to intercede on my behalf, and she said she did not want to suffer the same fate as me, so she would not intercede on my behalf. Knowing how vitriolic my kids were with me, I did not want my ex-wife to suffer the same fate, so I did not push her to say something to our children. Knowing that they control the power in the relationship shows how the kids are in charge of the kingdom; they are jangling the keys, and the estranged parents are accountable to them. The estranged are now secondary citizens in an up-side-down world.

A most troubling effect of estrangement is the absence of feedback from the adult child about what the parent did to deserve such a fate. If the adult child communicates what the parent needs to do to rectify their behavior, the parent/grandparent can improve. However, when there is no feedback from the adult child, there is no understanding of what needs to be fixed. Estrangement is a bullying technique: staying silent and not saying something to the estranged is the most humiliating and devastating thing a person can do to another human being. In other words, the parent/grandparent needs to be able to amend their ways by knowing what they are doing wrong. The cruelest effect of estrangement is the lack of feedback from the adult child, who refuses to listen and does not want to give a reason for ousting the parent from the family circle. Despite pleas to discuss the issue, the door was closed, and no conversation ever occurred about why the adult child was doing this.

Behavior in this manner will come back to haunt them when the parent passes away. Anything left unsettled between the adult and the child will haunt the adult child for the rest of their days, and actual therapy will have to occur. Losing relationships with family is as painful as losing them to an accident. Sometimes, a sudden loss leaves a child adult grieving because they did not take the time to engage the parent once they became adults. They may need to call the parents more or send cards on important parent holidays. Time passes quickly, and regretful children do not see the importance of maintaining a good relationship with a parent, whether the parent is perfect or not.

Another potential effect is perhaps the saddest part of this experience: getting to the point where one contemplates taking one's own life. In the course of my life, there was never anything that made me think of taking my own life, but this experience has. I imagined how I would do it to end my emotional pain. The pain was so great that I was not sleeping. I was unhappy, getting up in emotional pain and falling asleep in emotional pain. It was hard to deal with the pain. It was not until I got help from Dr. Joshua Coleman, whose books, articles, and seminars helped me find new meaning in my estranged life. The learning I did from his books and articles allowed me to write this book. I wrote this poem during this dreadful time to share how I felt about this devastating situation. I sent it to my ex-wife. I did not send it to my son and his wife or my daughter. If other communications did not make an impact, then this would also mean nothing. It means nothing to them.

Cause of Death: Broken Heart

And so the doctors came from far and wide with their stethoscopes,
Their lab reports, their X-rays, and their MRIs. The charts showed nothing
And they pondered and questioned each other and wondered how
Such a healthy man, who had no history of heart trouble, no cancers,
No blood work out of order, nor kidney failure or liver malfunction
Could go away without notice, without a good-bye, without cause.

They said he came from a normal family, had no history of premature deaths,
Parents and grandparents who lived long, lovely, and longed-for lives.
They said he never stopped working for his family nor let them down,
They said he never complained about caring for them when they were down.
They said he could have been better, but he did his best.

Doctors looked with all the tools of their trade, searched the medical journals,
They scoured the history of all those who came before, wondering aghast.
Their medical records had to show that life with this one had expired
For no visible reason, so they could only conclude the cause of death
To be just one thing: A Broken Heart.

Dad   2-1-21

As I said, this period was crushing for me mentally because it caused me to doubt my self-worth. My past actions for my family came into question, and all of the behaviors I performed as a father were doubted. This resulted from my son telling me that I was a narcissist. A narcissist is a person who thinks of no one except himself. After receiving his comment that I was a narcissist,

I wrote him a letter. I explained everything I had done for him while he was growing up. None of that mattered to him.

Also, the estranged find themselves in a powerless position. There is nothing a parent can do to change the adult child's decision. It will not be until the parent passes away that the decision to cut off the parent will be left in the lap of those who did such a thing. Let them deal with it for the rest of their lives. One of the regrets in life is to have unresolved issues with a parent, especially if that parent was a good one. Sometimes, people need to learn the hard way.

Finally, there is the anger one feels as a result of being kicked to the curb like a bum who doesn't deserve a second consideration. The anger is for many reasons; much comes from knowing how hard one worked as a parent to help the children become the best they could be. At the end of the book, I describe how my ex-wife and I worked very hard to make the best life for our children. The point is that despite those efforts, one can still manage to become an estranged person. It angers me when I think about all the hard work of being a parent, and then to be cast aside like an old used shoe is more than anyone can take. Even though one thinks of revenge, I learned that this social phenomenon is not my making but the making of a generation of indulged children. There would be no way I would even think of doing such a thing to my parents, much less exercise it.

There are additional damages to losing a relationship with an adult child and their grandchildren. Those I have discussed are what I have experienced throughout this tragedy. Estrangement is a silent, secret epidemic because few want to publicly display their "dirty laundry." So they keep quiet about it and don't tell close friends about their problems. The problem is an embarrassing one. The problem is full of shame. The parent or parents are telling their story to people who suspiciously think, "Okay, that is your side of the story," and so it goes. People don't trust someone who tries to tell their side of the "he said" and "she said" story. They want to hear the other side as well. As the reader will discover, this is my side of the story and the truth as I know it. I want to inform people as much as possible about the effects of such behavior and try to personalize the story of estrangement instead of writing an academic treatise. I hope my readers are those who have suffered the same fate and find solace in reading this account. Estranged people are not alone. Many have suffered the same fate.

Estrangement is a tragedy of epic proportions and the most significant "witch hunt" in American history. As Dr. Coleman indicates in the opening quote, no one knows who will be estranged and who will not be estranged. Bad parents have children who would never think of estranging them, yet many good parents see this happen to them all too often. Becoming estranged is like being identified as a "witch" in the early days of Salem, Massachusetts, in America in 1690. The designation of estrangement is no less damaging than being called a witch in Salem, Massachusetts. A frenzy of witches has been identified, and it will be some time before all the world is in good order again. American society is upside down, and it will take some work to set it back right side up again. In the meantime, many people have suffered what I have.

Chapter three informs us about what the research shows about the effects of estrangement. The research bears out the impact that estrangement has on estranged by the estrangers. In other words, what effects occurred to the estranged are those the research has proven to be true.

CHAPTER 3 :

What the Research Tells Us About the Effects of Estrangement

Elder abuse and child abuse are legal terms that would not be honored in an estrangement legal case used by the law, but many psychologists agree that estrangement is elder abuse and child abuse. According to Martin, she indicates that "Roberta Wasserman, LCSW-C, a therapist specializing in family estrangement, indicated that estrangement can be a 'devastating and traumatic experience. It is common for estranged individuals to feel profound sadness, anger, anxiety, guilt, and shame. The pain of estrangement is mainly due to having to grieve the loss of someone still around and the lack of closure. This is known as ambiguous loss, which lacks finality or closure. Ordinary loss and grief contain some elements of ambiguity, too. Estrangement is the temporary or permanent destruction of affection or alienation from our relatives. Although seldom named, it is a common motif in families. Sometimes, threads run through multiple generations of the same family" (Martin 1). Martin also states that "Wasserman suggests that one will be angry, have feelings of guilt, and suffer from anxiety, all of which happen at the same time. Estrangement can cause depression, anxiety, hopelessness, stress, suicidal ideation, and feelings of grief and loss." (Martin 1) So, the research backs up the personal feelings an estranged person has.

Sharon Widely tells us in her book *Abandoned Parents: The Devil's Dilemma* that "Frozen grief, frozen sadness, and ambiguous loss are often the words to describe the ongoing grieving state of the abandoned parent–a grief state that feels unmanageable. However, even those terms hardly describe the deep, soul-breaking pain that abandonment by your children can bring. The pain is fundamental, experienced on a cellular level, and imagined as beyond that which can be borne. Many of these abandoned parents harbor suicidal thoughts out of proportion to the general population." (44) Again, those who researched the complexity of feelings share what any estranged person will discover over time.

Widely says that "Abandonment leaves the parent outside the bounds of history. No one ever prepared the parents for this scenario. Preparation for future disasters is an essential part of family learning. What to do in case of drought, bankruptcy, job loss, and death is learned from our ancestors. It is family lore, stories of what was done when Uncle Bill died, how everyone survived the depression and victory gardens, and when the lightning struck the cherry tree. No one ever dreamed of being abandoned by their children. So there is no "story" to be told that gives abandonment perspective or wisdom to be shared or gives the aggrieved and hurting a place to stop the pain and start the healing" (45). In other words, all those estranged are left to deal with this situation without being prepared to deal with it. It can be a very troubling time, and it seems almost irresolvable. It is better understood with reading, and so I write to share with those who do not understand the deep, troubling feelings they are going through. When one understands the emotions of estrangement, getting a better grip on oneself is easier.

Again, in her book *Abandoned Parents: The Devil's Dilemma*, Sharon Wildey indicated, "First and let us be clear about this–parental abandonment is abuse, and it follows the model of other physical and psychological abuse. Most importantly, it is a moral and ethical failing on the part of the adult child. There may be a psychological diagnosis that can be made about the adult child who lives this hate-filled life and perhaps should be made, but first and above all, it is a moral failure. In some cases, even evil. Quite simply, it is the wrong thing to do, a wrong action to take, and places the adult child into a precarious environment that speaks to who they are, what they value, and the nature of their character. There is no crueler action to take against another human being than ostracism, abandonment, and alienation, especially when that other human being is your parent. What makes an adult child take such cold, calculating, and cultural norm action against the people who gave them life, support, and nurture in their minorities—people who fed them, educated them, protected them, and spent a good deal of the family resources to help them grow (Wildey 11)? This is an important question. What makes someone do something like this?

Every generation has had children abandon their parents for abusive behavior by the parent. There is nothing new in this respect, but unfortunately, parents regarded as outstanding parents are also receiving the same treatment. The internet has misled adult children, their psychologists, TV programs, and other sources. The current epidemic has fostered many books about the problem. Aside from the already mentioned books of Dr. Joshua Coleman, Karl Pillemer's book *Fault Lines: Fractured Families and How to Mend Them* has also received widespread attention. More personal accounts of this tragedy include Harriet Brown's *Shadow Daughter: A Memoir of Estrangement*. And there is Sharon Wildey's *Abandoned Parents: The Devil's Dilemma* and *The Invisible Grandparent* by Pat Hanson. Since I am not an expert on estrangement or a psychologist, my story is a personal look at what happens when adult children abandon their parent(s). It is no less important than academic writing. The last three books mentioned above are personal treatises on their experience with estrangement. This one is in a similar vein. Furthermore, numerous articles have been written about this problem, which has remained relatively quiet because of the shame associated with being identified as a "witch." Even though it is a silent epidemic, so much has been written that society has recognized estrangement as a significant problem.

In her book *Abandoned Parents: The Devil's Dilemma*, Sharon Wildey examines the effects of abandonment: "Society at large and their min-society of friends and family barrage these abused parents into a never-ending cycle of abuse by not even being able to imagine that children would viciously and systematically denigrate their parents unless those parents "did something wrong" or "there is always another side of the story," which is reinforced by the abusers, find a litany of rationalizations about how their parents "deserved" the ridicule, ostracism, and hypercritical conversations." (Wildey 59) Somehow, in their twisted mind, parents deserve to be treated in such a fashion. In my view, which is supported by Dr. Josh Coleman, when an adult child does this to a parent, it is just outright elder abuse—no question about it. Additionally, it is child abuse. The grandchildren are denied the right to love and care for a grandparent. Both Coleman and Wildey have indicated this is so many words.

As a result of being estranged, I drew some conclusions about the estrangers I want to share. Those who have been estranged may identify with my conclusions. This is the subject of chapter four.

CHAPTER 4:

What I Came to Conclude About Estrangers

I n this chapter, I want to distinguish my conclusions about the estranger. The estranger is the person or persons who do the estranging. They choose to eliminate the parent or parents or others from their lives for a variety of reasons we will eventually discuss. Although there are justified reasons for estranging someone, the estranger demonstrates characteristics of themselves through the process. While not all of these virtues are bereft in everyone who does estranging, these are some that are the result. These are my conclusions from my own experience, and it is important for both the estranger and the estranged to learn what they are.

ON FORGIVENESS

In Joshua Coleman's book *When Parents Hurt: Compassionate Strategies When You and Your Grown Child Don't Get Along*, he discusses the importance of forgiveness. He wrote, "Forgiveness doesn't mean you turn a blind eye to being mistreated by your children or others, or you never get angry. It doesn't mean you must have a relationship with the person who hurt you. Forgiveness doesn't mean you must accept, condone, or respect the behavior of those who have caused you to suffer. Forgiveness doesn't mean letting yourself off the hook for the harm you have caused without first making a heartfelt and significant effort to repair and make amends to the person you hurt." (Coleman 44) Coleman further states, "Forgiveness of yourself and others is important because it is a way of taking back your power." (Coleman 47) I have forgiven myself so that I can move on with my life. I have regained my power because I understand I am not entirely at fault. I cannot dwell any further on this matter. I have too much to do in my short time on this earth, and dwelling on whether anyone will forgive me is not in the cards. However, where is forgiveness when someone does something wrong?

The Bible, Genesis 50:17, says, "Forgiveness restores broken relationships." There can be no relationship without forgiveness. How can one ignore the apologies and not allow for forgiveness? Is it that someone was not taught that through religion? Even though I am not currently religious, I had a strong religious upbringing. I'm at least reasonable enough to know that when people make mistakes, they should be forgiven if they apologize for their mistakes. I made an outstanding effort to apologize for how I handled the situation. Yet, there was no forgiveness to be had.

In Luke 7:47, "Forgiveness is a path to love." How can our relationship be without love when I have done everything to establish that love with my family with my efforts with them? If there is no love, then there must be indifference. How can one live knowing that one is utterly indifferent to someone? Is indifference that close to the regions of love that one crosses over to the other side of the road at the first falling out of a relationship? What people do is honor indifference over love. How can one live with so much indifference in one's heart?

Forgiveness is so that the estranger can have peace of mind. According to Joshua Coleman, "Forgiveness of yourself and others is important because it is a way of taking back your power, taking responsibility for how you feel, and focusing on your healing." (Coleman 45) Forgiveness gives the estranger the ability to heal. It allows people to feel better about what transpired. It does not mean they must engage the parent again, but forgiving the parent is essential. I have met many people and read many accounts of people willing to forgive someone even for the most heinous act. I am tremendously disappointed in anyone's actions for not giving me another chance.

What also makes us human is the ability to forgive someone who has made a mistake. I watched a documentary about a family torn apart by the fact that the father had killed the mother in a fit of anger. After the trial, the children, who were adults in their 20s, went to see their father in prison to spend time with him. Even though they were distraught that their father had killed their mother, they saw him in prison anyway. An interviewer asked them why they would do such a thing. They answered that they were taught to forgive, put the past behind them, and move on with life.

ON COMPASSION

Compassion is the "sympathetic pity and concern for the sufferings or misfortunes of others." Knowing how painful it has been to be without my grandchildren, one would think one might have some compassion for the suffering of the estranged. Having compassion is demonstrating that one feels for the suffering of another. It appears that it does not matter how much a parent suffers when they are denied the chance to see and communicate with their grandchildren. How does one not know that it would be painful not to have grandchildren in one's life? It has to be a lack of compassion. I have learned that compassion is lacking when not responding to someone's pain.

ON THE MORAL AND ETHICAL WRONG OF ESTRANGEMENT

Turning one's back on the parent(s) is morally and ethically wrong. It is morally wrong because it is not how to handle family problems. It is just something that one should not do. It passes the boundary between right and wrong for someone to do.

It is ethically wrong because it is not the honest thing to do. It is a violation of proper behavior when conducting oneself with another person. When problems arise, turning one's back on them is not the right way to address them. Taking issues head-on is a more appropriate choice of behavior.

ON EMPATHY

In an article in HealthDay News, Amy Norton quotes the words of Joshua Coleman: "For any family reconnection to be healthy, Coleman said that a key ingredient is empathy–try to understand the other person's point of view." It would be nice to understand the other person's point of view if they are willing to express that view. Coleman also said in *When Parents Hurt:*

"Empathy is the ability to experience what others experience. It is the key to good relationships and social success because it gives an insight into what others think and feel" (87)

Empathy is the ability to understand and share the feelings of another. Although empathy can be learned, some people have a lower level of this skill than others. According to psychologists and researchers Paul Ekman and Daniel Goleman, there are three main types of empathy:

1. Cognitive empathy: This type of empathy is an intellectual understanding of someone else's feelings. It's the ability to consider other perspectives without sensing or experiencing them yourself. For example, if a colleague loses their job, you may recognize what emotions they could be feeling. You could also understand how their emotions might affect their behavior. This doesn't mean you experience distress yourself.

2. Affective or 'emotional' empathy: People with emotional empathy tend to feel another person's emotions. Although not always the case, this may include physical sensations consistent with such emotion. For example, if a person sees someone in great distress after losing a loved one, they feel sad themselves and could experience chest or stomach pain while sensing that emotion in the other person.

3. Compassionate empathy or 'empathetic concern': Compassionate empathy combines cognitive and emotional empathy. One recognizes and understands another person's emotions and also feels them. Taking on another person's challenges and hurt may take a toll on oneself. This is why some people may not develop this type of empathy. However, relating to other people's suffering may also lead one to consider getting help. Research suggests that when one gets help, the body produces more dopamine–a feel-good hormone. This motivates a person to continue acting on their cognitive and emotional empathy. Examples of compassionate empathy include stopping one's car to help if one sees someone fall or donating to a cause after a natural disaster.

Not everyone develops compassionate empathy, and there are also different emotional or cognitive empathy levels. For example, one could feel sad that one's partner is experiencing a challenge (emotional empathy). It hurts to see them hurt. Yet, one may need to understand *why* they feel this way. Or one may even feel that their reason for feeling sad isn't severe enough to warrant these emotions. One may have difficulty seeing the situation from their perspective (cognitive empathy). Because of this, one may not experience compassionate empathy.

There is no compassionate empathy when someone takes away the grandchildren from the grandparent. There is no understanding on the part of a person who does such a thing. Empathy is a characteristic that one either possesses or one doesn't possess.

ON HONORING THE MOTHER AND FATHER

The generations x and y following the Baby Boomers are not okay with honoring the mother and father.It is a consequence of the desire to have different values. Previous generations honored the mother and the father despite their inability to parent successfully. There is no such thing today. Honoring the mother and father isn't okay, even if the parents were good or even great parents.

"Honor your father and your mother, that your days may be long in the land that the Lord your God is giving you." (Exodus 20:12). Since some people have had little to no religious training, they may not realize that one of the Ten Commandments is to "Honor your father and mother," even if the parents aren't perfect. All people make mistakes, and that is what makes us human. There are no parents or grandparents who don't make mistakes when raising the children or engaging the grandchildren. To honor is to show respect for the person the parent is or was. To honor the parent is to keep a healthy relationship until they pass. I suppose there is no obligation on the part of some adult children to honor and respect a parent. This may be understandable if one was a bad parent or grandparent. Otherwise, it isn't.

It has been said that a parent loses nine years of life because of being rejected by the children. If the average age of men passing away here in the United States is seventy-eight years old, then I am just a few steps away from passing away. It is tough to accept that some people do not care if that happens. I am especially sad at knowing this potential outcome. I am sure this book will not change anyone's position. Christian morality teaches children to honor their father and their mother. But some people don't care about Christian morality. If they do not care about it, they do not honor it.

ON GRATITUDE

In her book *Daring Greatly,* Brene Brown, a renowned social scientist from the University of Houston, writes her "Wholehearted Parenting Manifesto," where she says, "I want you to know joy, so together we'll practice gratitude." Her family practices gratitude by bringing something each family member is thankful for to the dinner table. Brene also said that the "entitlement cure" is practicing gratitude. Gratitude can be learned in the home if the parents teach the children to be grateful for what they have. Gratitude can also be learned in the church and a religious setting. I was taught to say "thank you" to anyone who gave me anything because I got very little growing up. When a neighbor took us to the beach for a week to have fun in the sun and enjoy the waters of Doheny Beach, I was ready to go. When we returned, I stayed around and helped clean out the camper and all the stuff that was part of the trip. I helped wash the camper, too. The neighbor said I was the only one to say "thank you" for this beautiful trip. I was just expressing my gratitude for the great time this family offered us for a week at the beach.

When it comes to being grateful, nothing is more clear than Shakespeare as King Lear said in the play of the same name, "How sharper than a serpent's tooth it is to have a thankless child" (Act 1 Scene 4). One of the hardcore realities that parents come to learn is that gratitude for providing for their child's upbringing will be almost non-existent. Even though parents are not supposed to expect anything in return for their child's upbringing, isn't it acceptable to just be respectful of that effort? When a child turns his back on his parents, it is as if they are saying, "We don't care what you did for us when we grew up. We don't care about all the effort that you made for us. We just think it is normal to reject a parent for their behavior. That is just the way we are, and so accept it." And so I have.

Dr. Coleman reminds us in the book *When Parents Hurt: Compassionate Strategies When You and Your Grown Child Don't Get Along*, "Of all the principles, I believe that experiencing gratitude and seeking support are the most important. As Cicero wrote, 'Gratitude is not only the greatest of virtues but the parent of all of the others.'" (278). Learning to be grateful is to learn joy. I learned a lot about gratitude from this experience.

"But, what if they (the estranger) don't care about maximizing your well-being as a parent? What if all of your best efforts in the present and the past are being treated as though they have no value, and that you have no value as a person, let alone, a parent?" Josh Coleman indicates something that hits at the core of estrangement. All those efforts as a parent meant nothing to the adult children; parents are treated as if they did not do anything for their adult children, that they made no effort to support the family, or that the parent did not care for their welfare. Even though it isn't right to make an adult child feel guilty about this, it is still the feeling the parent has when one becomes estranged. Coleman reports that many parents are furious at their children after all they have done for them. Ultimately, it doesn't matter, and making them feel guilty about it won't change a thing. What they got in childhood is what they got, and they don't know anything different. I can contrast my childhood with my children's. And mine was a nightmare, and theirs was a trip to Disneyland. They don't care.

Finally, my friend Sue Krenwinkle had this to say about gratitude: "I particularly found the concept of gratitude a major aspect in possibly preventing abandonment. Raising children with the idea that the more you love them, the more they will be empowered to be stronger adults, especially if they never have to face failure, is not a good thing. An easy life is what we hope for our children, but not having consequences for poor choices can breed the narcissistic behavior that has made so many kids unable to have the tolerance to claim their part in a family issue that can cause a breach. If they perceive themselves always to be the victim, change seems an important aspect that is usually left for others to do, not them." Sue was a counselor for more than forty years, and her experience and insights were quite helpful to this book.

ON DEALING WITH ADVERSITY

"Coaches of children's sports activities began to give children trophies at the end of the season, regardless of whether they were on the losing or winning team. While parents before the twentieth century believed that the rigors of competition and strain would strengthen their children, contemporary parents began to fear that comparison with other children would leave them feeling insecure, discouraged, or damaged. Parents increasingly worried they weren't doing enough to develop and protect their children's self-esteem" (Coleman 66).

When a conflict arises in a family, it is measured in how they deal with it. In other words, when adversity comes in life, successful people work out a solution to the problem instead of ignoring the problem or running away from it. An unwillingness to address the problem demonstrates an inability to deal with the adversity thrown one's way. This is one of the fundamental things I have learned about estrangers from this experience. They don't address the problem but run away from it.

In *A Farewell to Arms*, Ernest Hemingway said, "The best people have the sense of beauty, the courage to take risks, the discipline to tell the truth, the ability to sacrifice. Ironically, their virtues make them vulnerable. They are often wounded, sometimes destroyed." Being vulnerable does not prepare a person for destruction, but those who show courage in the face of adversity are real heroes. People who throw themselves at the problem and solve it are who Hemingway would call heroes.

Even more to the point is the quote from Theodore Roosevelt that Brene Brown thinks is important for personal growth, "It is not the critic who counts: not the man who points out how the strong man stumbles or where the doer of deeds could have done better. The credit belongs to the man who is actually **in the arena**, whose face is marred by dust and sweat and blood, who strives valiantly, who errs and comes up short again and again, because there is no effort without error or shortcoming, but who knows the great enthusiasms, the great devotions, who spends himself in a worthy cause; who, at best, knows, in the end, the triumph of high achievement, and who, at the worst, if he fails, at least he fails while daring greatly so that his place shall never be with those cold and timid souls who knew neither victory nor defeat." Whoever is willing to take on a challenge after failure is the one who is seen as "daring greatly." When one does not solve issues because of the adversity one must face, then one is not daring greatly. One is giving up to the adversity in one's life.

The Millennial generation did not learn to fail because their parents would not let them fail. They got into the arena and learned that they would be victorious no matter what they did. When they meet adversity, they fall apart, shrink from the challenge, and demonstrate no courage in the face of adversity. One of the hallmarks of the Millennial Generation is that they grew up without failure. There were too many times when they lost the game and got the trophy anyway. (George Carlin and Jeff Dunham, both comedians, have been highly critical of this generation and the parents who rewarded the kids unnecessarily). The whole idea of awarding the players who were losers was a horrible move on the part of Baby Boomer parenthood in our day. Avoiding failure for the children was an effort to preserve their self-esteem. Avoiding failure resulted in creating a generation with enormous egos. The Baby Boomer generation created a generation of narcissists. They could do no wrong and were rewarded for it even if they lost. One cannot grow as a person without failure. Without failure, one cannot know success. Without failure, one cannot know how to deal with the adversity of it. When confronted with a problem in adulthood, they turned their heads and walked away from it. They cannot deal with problems, so they avoid dealing with them.

An adversity quotient is a score that measures a person's ability to deal with adversities in their life. As per W. Hidayat, the AQ (Adversity Quotient) also affects the students' understanding of mathematics. Hence, it is commonly known as the science of resilience. An adversity quotient is a person's ability to manage difficulties and transform obstacles into opportunities. The adversity quotient is one factor affecting a person's success since it correlates positively with their performance. Steven Jobs failed miserably but got back up and became a hero for Apple. He had failed as a student in college but learned how to succeed anyway by challenging the adversity in front of him. He did the same thing when he was fired from Apple at age 30. He got back up, reinvented himself, and became the incredibly successful man he was. He was a member of our generation, not the Millennial Generation.

ON THE NEED FOR ACCOUNTABILITY

A Chinese proverb is important to this entire book: He who blames others has a long way to go on his journey; he who blames himself is halfway there; he who blames no one has arrived.

There isn't a person who does not make mistakes as a parent or as a grandparent, but those mistakes should not be punished with estrangement. Even though the adult children choose to keep the grandparents from the grandchildren, isn't an effort to mend the wrongs better? Most of the time, when these situations occur, there are mistakes made by both parties. Isn't it necessary to take accountability for the mistakes each made in the disagreement? It is my observation that this was not exercised in my situation. Even though I was wrong to challenge the family about how my grandparenthood was handled, isn't it also the responsibility to accept the wrong committed on the other side? This is a failure of a generation that just does not see the importance of accepting responsibility when something goes wrong in a relationship. I apologized numerous times and said that I was wrong and accepted my part in creating the problem, but I did not get anything but four years of silence.

Most importantly, there is a need to take accountability for the mistake one has made. If there is no admission to doing wrong, there is no relationship. Admitting that one has made a mistake is paramount to making amends. Although it is never one person being right and one person being wrong, both sides must take responsibility for the estrangement. If one party does not take responsibility, then the relationship will not be mended. Both sides must be willing to say they are sorry for the misunderstanding and move forward. Estranging people in the family is a habit exercised too much since I am not the only one.

Again, my friend, Sue Krenwinkle, said this about accountability after reading my manuscript, "the book is a sobering reminder that the world of parenting has no magic formula, but accountability, on all sides of the equation, is necessary to meet problems early with honesty and direct dialogue. I learned the importance of recognizing that every family has its dynamics and that respect for reaching others and communicating about goals and expectations should be reviewed often. Family disagreements are not permanent when they can be resolved, mutually, with respect and forgiveness combined with the ability to accept accountability." Sue's insights came from her many years of experience as a counselor. They should be heeded to heal the relationship estrangers have caused.

Chapter Five will recount the need for the estranger to communicate the reasons for the estrangement. Giving the estranged some idea of what they did wrong is just a decent thing.

CHAPTER 5:

The Importance of Communicating a Reason(s) for Estrangement

I t is important for the estranger to communicate the reason(s) for estranging the adult parent or grandparent. First, isn't it decent to tell the parents or grandparents why they are being estranged? Don't they deserve an explanation as to why this is taking place? Is it appropriate to abandon the parents or grandparents and not give them any reason for this action? At least the parents or grandparents can know what they did wrong and perhaps rectify the problem. If the problem is not solvable, then let them know that it is not a solvable problem. It is better to do that than to leave the parent hanging without an explanation. Isn't it just plain decency to communicate the issue, and don't the parents or grandparents deserve that for being there for their children?

The more important reason for telling the estranged person(s) is so that they might have the opportunity to correct the behavior or apologize for not knowing what mistake they were making without their knowledge. Parents and grandparents are human, and they make mistakes. Isn't it fair to allow them to know what they did wrong that would warrant permanent banishment from the family? One can understand a temporary ban on any contact with the family, but a permanent ban without any explanation is just cruel and unusual punishment. I have read so many accounts of parents and grandparents who do not get told why they are being estranged. It is one of the reasons why they are so upset.

When the estranger communicates the concerns to the parents or grandparents, they can reflect on the problems they created. They at least know what to do with their behavior in the future. It gives them peace of mind knowing what they did wrong. It prevents them from speculating about what they did to deserve such a fate. It will allow them to sleep at night, knowing that something can be addressed to improve their relationship with the grandchildren and the adult children. It gives them time to reflect on what they can do to mend the fences. They can work to reestablish the relationship if given the chance.

Even though what the estranger might have to say to the parents or grandparents may not be something they want to hear, it is better than silence. Silence is unfair and cruel. Giving them a reason for the estranging allows them to respond to the accusations and present their point of view on the matter. Perhaps a parent or grandparent who has been abusive or unkind doesn't deserve a response. Still, those who have treated the grandchildren and the adult children respectfully should get some response to understand the adult child's actions.

A more important reason is that problems deserve the opportunity to be solved. Roadblocks in a relationship must be addressed so there is a clear path going forward. What good is a relationship without solving the problems before moving on to the next encounter? It is my understanding that many estranged parents and grandparents are often left without any explanation as to why they are being estranged. Oddly, a generation of people who would do this would not have wanted that approach used on them when they were growing up.

Reconciliation of a relationship can only occur with an opportunity to do so. The estranger needs to give the estranged an opportunity to redeem their behavior by indicating what must be done to improve the relationship. Why is it fait accompli that the estranger makes no effort to offer an opportunity to amend one's ways? A family counselor can handle the mediation of a relationship. Perhaps mediation can solve the crisis if given the chance. Complete abandonment without justification is bullying and cruel. Many psychologists call it elder abuse.

In chapter six, I discuss why grandparents are important to their grand-children. The next generation may not share that value, but the value of a grandparent can reach deeply into a grandchild's life.

CHAPTER 6:

Why Grandparents Are Important for Their Grandchildren

The millennial generation doesn't care about their elderly parents and subsequent grandparents. This is a generalized statement, but it may very well be true. Evidence seems to indicate that they don't, given the explosion of estrangement. Since grandparents are cast aside from any contact with their grandchildren, I suspect it is a pretty forgone conclusion that they don't think of them as necessary to their children's lives. So, I wrote this chapter to share with the estrangers what they might be taking away from the grandchildren when the grandparents are not allowed to interact with them. Here are some things that grandchildren benefit from when having the opportunity to interact with their grandparents.

A critical value of a grandparent is that "Grandparents might have artistic or intellectual interests that speak to the grandchild that differs from the parent." (Coleman 197). When I last visited my daughter's child, I learned of her artistic talent when I looked at all of the paintings and drawings she had done. I told her it was a "gift" from her great-grandmother, but a six-year-old has a tough time conceiving a great-grandparent when she has never seen a picture of her. I tried to share with my granddaughter that my mother was a good artist with different artistic talents. My daughter did not impede my communication about that to her daughter, but she also did not encourage the knowledge or the understanding of that family history. Knowing that these genetic traits and skills are passed from generation to generation, it should have been something that my daughter wanted her daughter to know. She was not excited about the idea, so my granddaughter probably did not think it was essential either. I also tried to tell my grandson that his athletic ability came from his great-grandfather, to my son, and then to him. Again, it is difficult to make an eight-year-old grasp the idea. How does that happen, Grandpa? Genetics. We all know that great athletes usually produce good athletic children if the mother and father are athletic. Sometimes, even a great athlete cannot make his offspring as athletic as he was, given that the child is the offspring of two people, not one. Letting the grandchildren know how they came to be as people is an important communication from the grandparents.

Also, a "Grandparent can create a foundation of safety, security, and identity whose removal may be deeply hurtful and disorienting to the grand-child." (Coleman 197). I wonder about the outcome of pulling me from my grandchildren and its effect on them. I had an excellent relationship with all three of my grandchildren, and it boggles my mind that they would pull them away from me because I objected to not being recognized as a grand-parent in an ancestry report. The grandparents need to teach the grandkids their identity and their ethnic make-up. Since I am a family historian, I was well-versed in being able to do that. I had some opportunities to teach them family history, but the most crucial time to discuss it with them has passed. And I have paid the price dearly for losing that opportunity.

Furthermore, "Grandparents can serve as a corrective to problematic or even traumatizing behavior from the parents." (Coleman 197) When I watched my son's behavior with his son, I saw a lot of angst between the two. His son was no angel and was often being scolded. I thought the parents were in for a lot of trouble when the child's teenage years arrived, and I am confident he will be highly rebellious since he displayed a lot of talk back to the parents at age nine. Sometimes, I took him aside and told him to respect what his parents asked him to do and to model good behavior. But the child was "dancing to the beat of his drum." Although one never knows if the grandparent impacts the child's behavior, it is essential to at least talk to the grandkid. During the time I spent with them, my son kept telling his son to listen. "You just don't listen." Well, perhaps the son is a "chip off the old block" since I had the same struggle with him when he was young but not quite as severe as his son. Once, I tried to get my son to chip a ball in golf like he putts a ball, but he was resistant to doing it that way. He wanted to do it his way. I told him to watch the best player and see how he does it. When he learned from the other players that chipping was a putting motion, he adopted it despite my teaching him the same way. It was his stubborn resistance and his stubbornness that I had to struggle with for a long time. Sometimes, a child is so different from what one expects that it is hard to believe that he is your kid, but as Dr. Coleman says, the parent tries to mold a child to his way of thinking when the child has a different way of thinking. This is what creates the conflict. We had our share of it. And so my son struggles the same way with his son; perhaps he is getting a taste of his own medicine. Yet, the grandparent can be a go-between between the parent and child. Without the grandparent, there is only conflict between child and parent that goes unresolved.

Moreover, Coleman suggests that Grandparents "can monitor problematic or dysfunctional family behavior and, where possible, intervene on behalf of the grandchild." (197). There were times when my son was pretty hard on his son, and when the disagreement was over, I would take my grandson aside and let him know that he is loved and a good boy. My grandson would be pretty angry at his dad for being so harsh, although sometimes he needed to be with his "dance to the beat of his drum" son. When a Grandpa can calm the feathers of his grandchildren with a few sage words, it means everything to a young child. It gives them a different perspective than the parent. My son does not see the importance of the grandparents during these problematic times. Estrangement has put the American family on their own when grandparents are kicked to the curb. Grandparents are unimportant.

Coleman also states that "...studies show that the relationship between grandparents and grandchildren is good for the well-being of the grandparent and children's development: grandparents can provide the grandchild with an important feeling of attachment, resulting in the grandchild's feeling more secure and loved." (Coleman 197) This bonding is essential to the child's development, yet too many of the Millennial generation do not regard this bonding as necessary to the child's development. This is tragic. I valued my small relationship with my grandparents, who impacted how I was as a person from the time I spent with them. For example, once, I was alone in the living room with my paternal grandmother, and she said, "They took my Steven." I said, "Who took your Steven, grandma?" She said, "The hospital took him." While I did not know who she was talking about at the time, I learned in my ancestry research that she had come to America after my grandfather (about a year later) and had three children with her. The youngest was Steven, who was less than a year old. He became ill on the ship and was dropped off at Hoffman Island, where he was quarantined with measles and other ailments. My grandmother never saw him again because she was processed through Ellis Island and was told that Steven had passed away from his disease. My grandmother's telling of this story inspired me to learn more about poor Uncle Steven and the origin of my family history. I did so and learned all the details of my grandparents' origin on both sides of the family. I believe that family history is essential and that knowing one's history is significant to understanding who we are. A grandparent must share this information with the grandchildren.

Grandparents also can serve as a rich resource of identity, history, and stories of family members. Because they are more invested in perpetuating the family lineage, they contain emigration stories, family recipes, clothing, and culture. Grandparents also provide a different role model of behavior for the child. They might have artistic or intellectual interests that speak to the grandchild that differ from the parent's. In short, grandparents can create a foundation of safety, security, and identity whose removal may be deeply hurtful and disorienting to the grandchild." (Coleman 197) As the family historian, I could offer my grandchildren a great deal of history about their great-grandparents and great-great-grandparents. These are best examined in light of my experience with my grandchildren. I have already shared an example of what I could have offered to my grandchildren. Ironically, as the reader will learn, I became estranged over an ancestry report that left me out as a grandparent. When my son said that his son did not make a mistake by leaving me out, I went on the offensive and told him that it wasn't right to do that since his wife had control over the report that I had edited two times. When I edited the report, it never mentioned grandparents. They were inserted into the report before my grandson's final presentation and ironically videotaped by my ex-wife, who posted it on Google Plus (now defunct). My current wife and I then just happened to see the video. The ensuing argument caused the estrangement. Although I have much to offer regarding family history, it is not essential to some Millennial generation.

Again, ironically, I became the family historian after I retired from teaching to determine once and for good what my exact ethnicity was. I learned that my four grandparents were all born in Slovakia and that I was a one hundred percent second-generation Slovakian. And even more ironic is that my daughter-in-law's mother is very much into ancestry and wanted to know the background and history of the Sinay name. I sent that history to her a long time ago. I also shared the history of the Sinay name with my son when I did the research in 2008 and had brief conversations with him about it. He was nonchalant and did not express much interest in it at all. I also tried to let my daughter know about Sinay's history, but I believe that she, like my son, did not care to learn about it. Perhaps it was due to the divorce, or perhaps because each of them does not care for my side of the family, or perhaps it is because they do not care about family history. Both of them only had two grandparents anyway. They were my parents.

It is poor thinking that grandkids cannot learn from their grandparents. I learned several things in my childhood from both sets of grandparents. I learned that it is vital to do a good job whenever one does anything. Grandpa Sinay taught me to cut the grass and trim the edges carefully. He taught me how to iron clothes and told me it was essential to get a good education. He taught me to have a good work ethic. He said that getting ahead requires one to work hard. I worked hard to get my education, and I worked hard as a teacher, both at the high school and college levels. Without question, one can learn much of lifelong importance from a grandparent. My mother's father, my Grandpa Labak, taught me to value many things and learned how to plant a garden. When I was going to college, he sent me a giant dictionary I used throughout my education.

I learned many things from my other grandparents, mother, and father. I learned about gardening, picking different vegetables, and picking strawberries. I learned how many other garden vegetables are grown in Granpa Labak and Granpa Sinay's backyards. I worked in those gardens, and I worked on the lawn. I learned to work. I learned a bit about the family's history from Grandpa Sinay and about being nice to grandkids and having them remember me as nice to them. Grandparents can be a source of great and positive influence on the lives of their grandchildren. I believe that no matter what, my grandchildren will remember me as a good grandpa despite their parents' choice. Grandparents are very important to the lives of their grandchildren.

Coleman says, "Our culture's disdain of aging reveals itself in the little regard accorded the role of grandparents when conflict occurs. Grandparents are viewed as one more relationship to be disposed of when they don't satisfy the criteria required to sustain parent–adult-child relationships. **I have worked with far too many families where the grandparent is cast off because of conflict between the child or their spouse and the parent.** This is true even when the adult child acknowledges that the grandchildren love the grandparent." (198) That sums up my situation. It did not matter that the grandchildren loved their grandpa; my son and his wife cast me off like I had leprosy. I had established an excellent relationship with my grandchildren, yet they disregarded my importance to their development. It did not matter that I did ninety percent of things right with them; I got booted for ten percent of what I did wrong. If a family cannot forgive the mistakes of a grandparent, then our society is doomed.

Again, Coleman comments on this situation, "Curiously, a generation that has redefined what should be considered abusive child-rearing behavior is so casual when casting a grandparent out of their children's lives. For a generation obsessed with closely hewing to theories on attachment between themselves and their children, it is remarkable how many seem to disregard their children's profound attachment to their grandparents." (197) The generation who values close ties with their children thinks casting off a grandparent is not wrong. This is just pure ignorance when a grandparent is cast aside, and no consideration is given to their children's mental health. This generation has little understanding of grandparents' profound connection to their grandchildren. The lack of consideration for the importance of a grandparent doesn't phase this generation. Yet they have no problem doing it even when they think they are doing it for the good of the grandchild. Some psychologists call this child abuse.

Coleman continues, "And while this is often framed as a healthy life setting for the grandparents, one has to wonder, How healthy could it be? Is it good modeling to so prize your feelings that you'll sacrifice your children's relationship on the altar of that aspiration? Is it a strength to not be able to separate your child's needs from your own? Does it model healthy separation to assume that your children's mental well-being is so tied to yours you can't imagine that your children benefit from a relationship with your parents, even if you find it upsetting or difficult? What does that teach children about the value of older people and what they might contribute to life or society?" (198) What does this teach the children when grandparents are cast aside as if they have died? I wonder if my son and his wife think that they are teaching the children to do this to them. What lesson have they taught the children that will return to haunt them in their old age—that casting aside a grandparent is okay? Haven't the parents modeled this for their children so they can expect the same treatment when their children have children? Did they even once consider the effects that this has had on their children? Finally, Coleman asks, "What does it teach a child about the value of older people and what they can contribute to their children's lives?" (Coleman 198). They have taught their children that older people are not valuable, grandparents are expendable, and there is no purpose to them.

"I often hear estranged grandparents describe the loss of their grandchildren as even more painful than the loss of their adult children. They describe the love for a grandchild as more raw and pure, its disappearance more disorienting and bewildering, the need to reconnect with the grandchild more desperate and vital." (Coleman 208)

Losing contact with the grandchildren is devastating and enormously hurtful. In this chapter, I tried to show how important grandparents can be to the lives of their grandchildren. From my experience, I know the influences of both sets of grandparents were significant to my life. Although I only had twelve years of my life with my grandparents, it was enough to influence me positively. I learned good things from my grandparents; they are a valuable and necessary part of a grandchild's life.

In Chapter 7, I suggest what reasons are unjustified for estrangement. These reasons are unjustified because many problems are solvable with good communication or family therapy.

Unjustified Reasons for Being Estranged?

I t is important to point out the experience of an established expert on estrangement, Dr. Joshua Coleman, who stated in *Rules of Estrangement: Why Adult Children Cut Ties and Heal the Conflict*: "So let me start by saying maybe you didn't do anything to cause it. While there are plenty of troubled parents in this world, many of those who contact me are some of the most dedicated, educated, and loving parents of any generation" (2).

This chapter is more about reasons outside the parent's control, and falling into an area a parent isn't fully responsible for. Truthfully, those reasons might include a disagreement over how the grandchildren should be disciplined, how the grandchildren should be fed, or how the grandchildren should be treated. They also include disagreements over matters in the family, presents given to the grandkids, or comments made to the grandkids that don't meet the parent's approval. These estranger adult children who find the oddest reasons to oust a parent or grandparent are those who make their own mistakes with their children but don't see the double jeopardy in their treatment of the parents or grandparents. Some of these basic mistakes made with a grandchild constitute the source for many of the unnecessary estrangements in American society. Adult children might perceive their child being treated in the same way they were when they were young, and consequently, the adult child will not have it, and estrangement follows.

Is it possible to estrange parents or grandparents over what they feed the grandchildren? It is, and it has been done. I start with this cause for estrangement because it shows how absurd the reasons are for throwing the parents or grandparents to the curb. I have read about such cases, and one wonders why there is no solution to that problem instead of ostracizing the old folks. In other words, how come there isn't a reasonable solution to the issue, and then the family can move forward?

Another situation that sometimes warrants estrangement is disciplining the grandchildren the same way the adult child was disciplined. This situation was another one that came into my reading about estrangement. Why don't the adult children just communicate how they would like to see the kids disciplined when they are under their care? Although this may seem silly, it is not silly to generations X, Y, and Z. They take their parenting seriously but are really about as clueless about parenting as most generations. What manual do they use? It appears they give little regard to how they were raised. One of the saddest things happening in estrangement is that good and even great parents are victims of estrangement for reasons like those just discussed. Again, Coleman states "But I've worked with hundreds of people who have been good–or good enough–parents and don't deserve this type of treatment" (210).

Another disconcerting reason for estrangement is parents' excessive involvement in their children's lives. In the same *Atlantic Magazine* article, Dr. Joshua Coleman states, "Estrangement is born from love. One of the downsides of the careful, conscientious, anxious parenting that has become common in the United States is that our children sometimes get too much of us–not only our time and dedication but also our worry and concern. Sometimes, the adult child needs to leave the parent to find themselves." The problem of being a "helicopter parent" forces some adult children to seek separation from the parent(s) due to too much care and love in the growing child's life. The estrangement is the reason for separating from those who spent too much time with their children when they were growing up. This partly makes the adult child want to separate from the parent. The adult child has already had too much of the parent earlier in life and wants to shed them in adulthood. Because Baby Boomer parents were the first generation to exercise "helicopter parenting," they are the first recipients of estrangement for unjustified reasons.

Getting too much of a parent did not happen in the Baby Boomer generation. When I was growing up in the 1950s, our lives as children were on our own. When we got home from school, it was out the door to play until dinner and back out the door until it was time for bed. We did not have parents hovering over us on a day-to-day basis. There was no such thing as a "helicopter" parent. Unfortunately, after excessive involvement with the child, the now adult child is looking for separation and not more contact with their parent. Coleman continues, "Many fathers and mothers feel betrayed by their children's lack of availability or responsivity. Especially those who provided their children with a life they see as desirable compared with their childhoods." Indeed, this would be the case with my ex-wife and my parenting: we were very involved. Ironically, Millennial parents are highly involved with their children, and the consequences of their "helicopter" behavior are already showing the same consequences in Generation Z.

Interestingly, Generation Z also rejects their parents because of their excessive involvement with their children. Generation Z may be rejecting parents more than Millennial adult children. In the same article, Coleman indicates that "Parents expect a 'reciprocal bond of kinship' in which their years of parenting will be repaid with later closeness." with the adult child. However, the expected involvement with the adult children often leads to conflict and the resultant estrangement. Disagreements result in estrangement because the adult children want the separation from the parent(s).

One of the main reasons for estrangement is divorce. In this regard, it happens to both good and bad parents. Even though some divorces are so nasty that resolutions cannot be made, most divorces can have reasonable solutions to continue to have a friendly relationship. Statistically, about 70% of estrangements happen due to divorce, according to a study done by Joshua Coleman. One thousand four hundred estranged parents were asked to relate what they thought the cause of the estrangement was, and divorce led to the causes more than anything. Divorce separates a parent from the family. Most of the time, it is the father who becomes estranged from the family. Coleman has indicated that "Divorce can create a radical realignment of long-held bonds of loyalty, gratitude, and obligation to the family (201). Divorce causes family members to spin further and further out of one another's reach. This can be the basis for estrangement.

For some divorces, the spouse of the estranged is the reason for the estrangement. The spouse is so angry that they denigrate their ex by showering the children with their one-sided version of the marriage. When the children are left to the devices of the parent left alone, often they turn their anger on the parent who has left and twist the understanding of the marriage in the children's minds. The children resent the parent who has left the family, which helps foster estrangement. I knew a father who left his wife for another, and the two boys of the family sided with the mother and supported her grief. The father had a strained relationship with the children and rarely saw them. When a man leaves his wife for another woman, it exacerbates the problem. Thus, divorce can bring about a separation from the parent who left the family. When the children are left at home with the spouse, they are a captive audience for the spouse to spout off about the other parent. It happens all the time.

Another disturbing reason for estrangement is that the adult child feels "entitled" to do so. They may do it, as they claim, for their "happiness" or to avoid what they call "pain" caused by the parent. Being "entitled" to estrange a parent has been identified as the reason for the epidemic: almost any reason qualifies to dump the parent or grandparents from the lives of the adult child and his children. In an article in *The Economist* Magazine entitled " How Many American Children Have Cut Contact With Their Parents?" Coleman comments on one of the guiding factors: "A rise in individualism that emphasizes personal happiness is the most significant factor. People are increasingly likely to reject relatives who obstruct feelings of well-being in some way by holding clashing beliefs or failing to embrace those of others. Personal fulfillment has increasingly come to displace filial duty. In other words, if the parent is not making the adult child happy, then that is the reason for abandoning the parent. It is more important for the adult child to secure their happiness over a filial obligation to the parent. This rise in individualism can be characterized by three words: me, myself, and I." In short, what is essential to the adult child is far more important than worrying about a relationship with a parent who provided them with everything they needed to succeed. A family obligation is not an essential value to the Millennials, as will be discussed later in the book.

Another cause of estrangement happens because the adult children will be happier without the parent. While this may be true for an adult child who has suffered a great deal of abuse while living at home, it is also one of the main reasons adult children of the Millennial generation throw their parents under the bus. Perhaps the adult child has had too much of the parents and wishes to break free of them. In an article in *Atlantic Magazine*, "A Shift in American Family Values is Fueling Estrangement," Dr. Coleman writes, "Our American love affair with the needs and rights of the individual conceals how much sorrow we create for those we leave behind." In other words, the adult children are looking for more personal happiness at the expense of casting off the unworthy parent(s). The Millennial generation says, "We may see cutting off family members as courageous rather than avoidant or selfish. It is better to 'go it alone' than do the work to resolve conflict." In other words, this generation has no time to resolve conflicts with their parents because they are too busy with their individual needs. The shift toward individualism has exploded, a significant cause of estrangement.

Moreover, geographic distances foster estrangement. In an article in *The Economist* magazine, Dr. Coleman comments, "America remains one of the most geographically mobile countries in the world. The vast distances often involved allow people who want to leave their families behind to do so." With this distancing of families, poor communication results from more complex communication with separate time zones. Over time, this distancing can cause misunderstandings, and with that sometimes comes total separation. In other words, as families have separated to distant parts of the country, communication has declined, resulting in a permanent separation.

The literature written by psychologists has become a justification for estrangement, Dr. Coleman also states that "Those who decide to break off contact with their parents find support in a growing body of books (often the word "toxic" is in the title) as well as online." Coleman has indicated that too many psychologists are giving adult children the right to estrange a parent or parents when they consider them "toxic." This is a word bandied about by too many psychologists who feel that children who have reached adulthood can toss away a parent if they find them too toxic for their world. Perhaps the Millennials have read something along the lines of getting rid of their "toxic" parents. It has been described as one of the causes of this social phenomenon of tossing parents out of their lives.

Coleman continues in the same article, "Threads on internet forums for people who want to break ties with their parents reveal strangers labeling people they have never met as narcissistic or toxic and advising an immediate cessation of contact. This may make it easier to shelve feelings of guilt." Sadly, as the reader will learn later in the book, this is precisely what happened. Instead of resolving the issue, my son resorted to name-calling he found on the internet and used it as a basis for deciding to estrange me. Perhaps I became "toxic" to him and his wife, but for thirteen years after I divorced, I was not toxic and babysat the kids at several locations.

One potential cause is that the internet is filled with information that can be misleading. I was told that I was a narcissist because my adult child "looked it up." Information spewed by therapists in their articles about estrangement is often misleading and urges adult children to eliminate or remove the "narcissistic" or "toxic" parents from their lives. And so they do. They toss the parent(s) to the curb and never want them back into their lives. This is one of the central reasons for good parents having to endure estrangement.

Another unintended cause is disagreements between the parent(s) and the son-in-law or daughter-in-law. The in-law no longer wants the parent to be part of their family and urges the adult child to discard the parent(s). In this case, the estrangement has more to do with the feelings of the in-law than it has to do with any egregious behavior on the part of the parents. Sadly, the disagreement may not be serious but sufficient enough to merit estrangement. Sometimes, the disagreement can be even trivial like getting the wrong kind of present for the child's birthday or saying something inappropriate about the child's behavior.

Sometimes, parents can be unwilling to accept the reality of a son or daughter coming out gay. This problem is the unwillingness of the parent to accept their child as a gay person, so they become estranged for that reason.

Associated with this situation is a child wanting a sex change operation that just defies understanding by the parents. This situation also leads to the same result: estrangement.

More than anything in the last several years, politics has divided families like never before. The political divide has families uncomfortable with their choice of leadership, especially with the election of Donald Trump. Instead of unifying the country, he further divided it with his overreach in decision-making. Parents and children have lost contact over this problem at an alarming rate. Discussions at the Thanksgiving table about politics became impossible, and many estrangements resulted from the political divide.

In an article on webmd.com, Josh Coleman has indicated that estrangement is not reserved for standard reasons. Estrangement is also happening to those parents who are considered good, if not great parents, by his standard, and there are hundreds of them he has treated who are suffering this fate. Why is this happening to parents who are considered to be good parents and not parents who qualify for being estranged by children who have been abused in some way or another? The answer is difficult to understand because many of those doing the estranging will not even tell their parents why they are doing the estranging. From my reading and experience as a parent who was far above standard in performance, I want to share some speculative causes for this occurrence.

Although the causes of estrangement are multiple, an exhaustive investigation of them is not the purpose of this book; instead, a brief understanding of those causes pertinent to the estrangement situation has hopefully enlightened the reader. These causes fall more into the unjustified category because there are solutions to them that all parties can respect. It is getting the parties to work together to devise solutions to the estrangement rather than perpetuating it.

In chapter eight, I discuss why bad parents are estranged and why it is justified. Learning these justifiable reasons will let estrangers know that they are victims of these egregious behaviors and that estrangement is sometimes necessary. There is a distinction between justifiable reasons and those that are arbitrary.

CHAPTER 8:

Justified Reasons for Being Estranged

According to Coleman, "Some parents are responsible for transgressions that are harmful to their children: child abuse, incest, neglect, and alcoholism are a few of the more egregious examples" (21). These are discussed in this chapter to let those who have estranged parents as a result of these abuses that they are justified in doing so. However, some commit such acts and are willing to make amends if given the chance, and those who are willing to do so may find a willing adult child to mend their differences.

Dr. Sharon Martin, an online therapist with the website "livewellwith-sharonmartin" cites why adult children estrange their parent(s) based on the research. She states that "Research indicates that adult children most cite abuse, betrayal, indifference or lack of acceptance from their parents as the reasons for their estrangement (Agllias, 2016; Carr et al., 2015; Conti 2015; Scarp et al., 2015). For example, in a study conducted by Carr et al. (2015), adult children attributed estrangement to parent "toxicity" (defined as cruel, hurtful, or disrespectful treatment from a parent), feeling unsupported and unaccepted, or abuse perpetrated by the parent or a lack of support when the child was abused by someone else." (Martin 1) Since estrangement has always been a part of each generation, it is important to note that much of what has happened in the past probably constituted justifiable estrangement.

Each and every generation before has had children estrange their parents for mistreatment. First, let's take a look at those egregious causes of estrangement that Dr. Martin is outlining.

There is sexual abuse, a parent taking advantage of one of their children. Perhaps one of the most egregious acts is to make sexual advances on children. There are laws to protect children from such behavior, and the law usually takes the child out of the family setting before too much damage is done. Dr. Martin indicates that "Agllias (2016) found that adult children cut ties with their parent due to abuse (Physical, emotional, sexual, or failure to protect), poor parenting (an authoritarian parenting style, parentification, or lack of support), and betrayal (lying, embarrassing the adult child, or sabotaging or undermining their other relationships). Also, if a parent is accused of indifference to the child or an inability to accept the child. Moreover, adult children cite the "toxicity" of the parent, which is defined as cruel, hurtful, and disrespectful treatment, a feeling of being unsupported and unaccepted, and not having any support when another adult abuses a child.

Another egregious cause that qualifies as abusive is physical abuse. Physical abuse was why Huck Finn wanted separation from his father. Any child is protected today from physically abusive parents if the child is willing to communicate the abuse to an authority. There were times when I had to send students to the counselor's office when I determined that physical abuse was taking place in the home. When Huck is kidnapped by his father, he takes him to a cabin near the river and locks him in. Huck is then physically abused by his father with the belt, and the result is just horrific on the back of Huck. Although Twain was not making a statement about parental abuse, he did show how horrific it can be.

Aside from the physical abuse, there is emotional abuse, and often, a child will withdraw and demonstrate behavior that beckons questions to the student. Students who are emotionally abused are usually called names by their parents. I know of a family where the father would always call his children stupid because he wanted to feel superior to them. Huck Finn's father is jealous that Huck is becoming educated, and he does not care. Parents who degrade their children are emotionally abusing them, and over time, a child is justified in not wanting a relationship with the parent. On the other hand, my generation treated many in this fashion, yet our generation did not think of shedding our parents.

Estrangement comes as a result of excessive drug or alcohol abuse. Alcoholic parents are abusive to children out of neglect. Parents who find that it is more important to drink than care for their children are more numerous than we want to know. I know of a couple who had three children who constantly found both parents either too intoxicated or incapable of proper care. When the children became adults, two of the children drank excessively while one maintained the right distance from it. The parents did not lose the children to that behavior, and the children did not abandon their parents because of it. Yet, the closeness of the family was not there. Then there is drug abuse that also brings about the need to estrange the parent. Since drugs are so prevalent in our society, it is not unusual for parents to lose the battle to them. The children grow up learning the wrong thing and find their way out of the home and out of that environment as soon as they can stand on their own two feet.

Martin supports the idea of value differences by saying, "Estrangement may also be related to parents and adult children having differing values (Agllias, 2015; Gilligan et al., 2015). This makes sense as we are experiencing greater ideological extremes and political divides. For some, family relationships become untenable when their values and beliefs are attacked, or family members are unwilling to respect their boundaries (such as a request not to discuss certain topics or not to disparage the other person for having differing beliefs)" (Martin 2).

Politics has been a great family divider, especially over the last several years, where the divisions have been so great. People have been inundated with false information and they have ascribed themselves to conspiracy theories so that the children cannot accept the bizarre beliefs of the parent. So they become estranged as a result of that. As I write this, a family member is making statements about the current political situation. One wonders if someone like this realizes the damage done to family over political nonsense. However, the divide over this issue has grown exponentially over the last ten years and has caused family divides like we have never seen before. Although this may not be a reason for estrangement, sometimes separation is needed.

Adult children often cut ties with their parents as a way to protect themselves from further harm. Parent and child relationships can go well when there is respect for the child. Estrangement can occur when a breach in that relationship over a perceived disrespect. One can understand if the relationship was abusive. Parents who subject their children to these behaviors often have them estrange themselves from the family because they are tired of dealing with such behavior. Indeed, there are reasons why some adult children are justified in estranging their parents.

Perhaps most importantly, estrangement occurs because the nuclear family has dissipated in American society over the last fifty years. We have only one-third of our families that have two natural parents. The rest are an assortment of one family intertwined with another. Often, this is a recipe for disaster, and estrangement has happened due to the breakup of the nuclear family.

PART II:

FOR THOSE WHO HAVE BEEN ESTRANGED

This section is for those poor souls who have been estranged, and the purpose is to offer some solace to them. Some forces bigger than the individual parent have brought about the estrangement crisis. The whole estrangement crisis is pretty complicated, and it has evolved from generation to generation. Generations typically "thumb their noses" at some of the conventions of previous generations, and therein lies the conflict. More significantly, the rise in individualism in America has brought about the consummate "It's All About Me" generation. These chapters are to let those who have been estranged know that it is not the full fault of the estranged that finds them in this situation, but it is as much the fault of the estrangers.

CHAPTER 9:

Why Good Parents Are Not Responsible for Estrangements

I n his book *When Parents Hurt: Compassionate Strategies When You and Your Grown Child Don't Get Along,* Coleman informs us that "While some parenting behaviors can create problems in children, I believe we need a much more nuanced and complete picture than the one currently being provided by therapists, politicians and talk show hosts. A larger picture is necessary because influences such as genes, economics, peer groups, siblings, culture, and personality can cause some kids to make their mediocre parents look and feel pretty great while others make their exceptional parents look and feel pretty awful. Some children, just by their nature, create a lot of parental error and heartache. Some environments create problems in children that have little to do with whether mom and dad are following the latest and greatest parenting advice to a T"(8,9). This chapter will address the issues that are out of the control of the parent, such as the genetic predisposition, their peer groups, their siblings, their culture, their personality, and their economics.

When our children were young, my ex-wife was reading books about how to deal with a stubborn child. It was about our son's behavior. It did not do a great deal of good. If someone is genetically predisposed to stubbornness, an alternative approach to parenting such a child will not work. As Coleman says, "Some children, just by their nature, create a lot of parental error and heartache." (Coleman 9) The reader will learn that even perfect parenting cannot affect the elemental genetic composition of a child. If a child is cantankerous, it is not the result of parenting but of the child's fundamental nature. If a child is unruly, then a parent cannot change that. If a child has ADD or Attention Deficit Disorder, the parent can not change that. ADD may be controlled with drugs, but perfect behavior does not often result, and the long-term physical problems associated with Adderall, the drug for ADD, are well documented. In short, genetic predispositions trump parental training. It is nature over nurture.

A fine example from my own family is this: one can do nothing about a child's ADD or Attention Deficit Disorder. It was a genetic "gift" from the mother's side of the family. The uncle, the mother's brother, was the worst case of ADD I had ever seen in my thirty-seven-year career as a teacher. In a conversation with him one time, we covered sixteen subjects in a matter of five minutes. He once made fun of me because I could not keep up with the shifting subjects he discussed with his sister, my ex-wife. And if one could not keep up with his shifting of topics approach to discussing something, he would insult the person. He was very good at insulting people. A person with ADD does not focus on one subject for any length of time because it is not in their genetic makeup. Fortunately, the gene was not ADHD or Attention Deficit Hyperactivity Disorder, a more debilitating condition. I had several students with both conditions in my long teaching career. They were some-times challenging to deal with. I am sure these are examples of how a child behaves from their DNA makeup.

Therefore, genetics is the first and most important influence on estrang-ing a parent by an adult child. Coleman states that "this research shows that about half of the way that children behave has nothing to do with the quanti-ty of affection and active listening and stimulating environment that we pro-vide, and a lot to do with that bodybuilder, DNA, tells it to." (16) The truth about DNA comes out prominently when parents decide to adopt. Adopting a child is picking out a child from a DNA grabbag unless the adoptive par-ents know the details of the birth parent(s) background.

One must consider what happens sometimes when parents adopt a child. They do not know the genetic background of the child's parents, al-though they may learn some background of the parents. Even though they may try to shape the adopted child's behavior, the child just "dances to the beat of a different drummer, " which is their genetic makeup. For example, my younger brother adopted two children. Both of the children came from different parents and had different backgrounds. My brother and his wife are highly religious, and both felt that with proper religious "training" and learning from the Bible, the children would grow up to be healthy, happy, and responsible adults. The boy was adopted when he was four years old, and by the time he was six, he was making life difficult for them. One time, when his family came to our house, the child pulled out a knife and proceeded to carve his initials on a sliding board in the park near our house. He was already showing dangerous behavior at this young age. His birth parents, both in prison for various crimes, were the genetic background of this child. The child grew up and, over the years, caused considerable angst in the family. My brother and his wife were ready to call the marriage quits because of the stress of having an incorrigible child. No religious passage could circumvent the genetic predisposition to be threatening and mischievous. The same child stole money from his parents and their work locations. He was difficult. Fortunately for my brother and his wife, the child left home at sixteen and has not been a part of the original family since. The troubles the child caused my brother and his wife are too numerous to delineate. The point is made: nature thrives over nurture. DNA trumps biblical lessons.

Another example of nature thriving over nurture comes from the same family; the other adopted child was a girl. The young lady they adopted had genetic issues almost immediately; the birth parent, knowing that the child was going to be a problem, gave the child up for adoption. The child was obese almost from the time she was five years old. That never changed; she died young due to a diabetic condition. Although she was not a significant problem with the family when she lived with them at home, she could not care for herself. She was a victim of her genetics. Although her parents greatly impacted her, she could not care for herself. She passed away by herself without managing her physical problems. Genetics dictated her life and not her parental environment.

My oldest brother had an incorrigible son. His son broke ties with his father when his mother died of cancer in her late thirties. He then blamed his father for the death of his mother, and they had a very strained relationship for the rest of their lives. Although he was not entirely estranged from his father, it was close to that. However, as time wore on, he treated his father like he was an outcast. My brother passed away at age 76 without resolving his son's conflict with him. It is hard to know how and why a person treats his father in that manner, but I completely understand it from a genetic point of view. The son had some qualities that were not like his father and more like his mother's family. The son also greatly regretted his treatment of his father after he passed away. But it was his son's fundamental nature that allowed him to treat his father so disrespectfully when he was alive.

My sister had a similar fate with her son, who created problems for her when he was at home and after he was married and divorced. His problem was drugs and alcohol, driving deplorable behavior, and poor responsibility. Again, these are two examples of young adults who allowed their behaviors to supersede the excellent parenting of both my brother-in-law and sister. It was not until his late 40s that the son found a good woman who had kept him in good stead for several years. The son had behaved the same way as his father did even though the father was never in his life. His father took drugs and made a mess of his life as well. The apple doesn't fall far from the tree.

A friend of mine has been left helpless by the behavior of his oldest son, who sought out drugs instead of seeking a career path. Even though his sister is quite successful, both are products of the same good upbringing of the two parents. Although the parents are the kindest people anyone might ever want to meet, they have a son who has caused them more trouble than a team of wild horses. It is time to recognize that adult child behavior is more than the child's upbringing by the parents. Children's paths are often guided by their own genetics.

Another friend adopted a girl who was a childhood challenge and an adult challenge for who knows how long. She finally righted the ship in her early 40s and has an admirable relationship with her parents. Again, the delinquent behavior resulted from not-so-gifted genes that made school challenging and a good education impossible. Without an education, supporting oneself is a struggle, and it has been for years for this young lady. The parents were both well-educated but incapable of controlling the wanton behavior of their adoptees. Again, nature triumphs over nurture.

Dr. Coleman makes that point by saying, "The recent findings in child development and genetics are relevant because they show that children come into the world springloaded for action far more than anyone previously thought." (Coleman 15). This means that kids already have predispositions to act in a certain way. This is one of my main arguments in the book. A parent cannot accept responsibility for a child's behavior when he was prewired to behave that way. The genetic composition of any child is that of the mother and the father. The result may be that one child is more like the father, and the other child is more like the mother, not only in personality but also in genetic construction. However, half of the genetic composition constitutes how a child will be despite the training by the parents. So, parents and adult children of those parents, take note. Parents cannot be fully responsible for the behavior that comes from their children if that behavior is an undesirable trait. It is simply DNA. If the child is stubborn, the child acquired the trait from somewhere in the genetic past. Sometimes, we punish ourselves too much for the adult child's behavior when their behavior results from who they are genetically. Even the best parenting cannot overcome that.

Additionally, the child's personality may be such that they are just incorrigible and that cooperative behavior with the parents is impossible. When the child develops a problematic behavior, it can be more the result of the given personality rather than the training of the parents. Parents do not form the child's personality, although their personality comes from the makeup of both parents. A person's personality is unique to them, and that construct cannot be reshaped by the parent or by any other means. It is the same problem as the "conversion" theory of stopping a child from being gay.

Another reason why parents cannot take responsibility for this estrangement epidemic is because it is a social phenomenon. Estrangement has happened because a significant generation has decided that their happiness is more important than filial responsibility. The Millennial Generation (and certainly not all of them, but a significant portion) has decided that casting off their parents is a healthy thing for their happiness. Perhaps that segment of that generation just got too much of the parents and wants them banned from their sight. Getting too much of a parent leads to consequences in the adult child's life. They simply did not want more of the parents because they already had too much of them. While the Baby Boomer generation went about playing outside until the street lights came on, the Baby Boomer parents were hovering over the children during that same period in the child's life. It wasn't bad parenting, but it was excessive parenting, "helicopter" parenting as it has been called. Whatever the reality, it is essential to know that the choice to be estranged is not that of the parent. Members of our generation would just not think of ostracizing a family member. Although estrangement may have happened in our generation, it was because it was the adult child's choice that probably came as a result of abusive behavior. Parents in the Baby Boomer Generation did not oust their parents because they were tired of them, mostly because they did not get a lot of them growing up.

Another more formidable reason Baby Boomer parents are not responsible for estrangement is that Millennials are more concerned about their happiness than filial responsibility. Millennials believe it is more essential to oust a parent than to resolve the conflict. It is more vital for them to turn to their efforts at being happy, including ousting a parent or parents. This is demonstrated by the fact that many well-meaning parents are also a part of this social phenomenon of estrangement. As Josh Coleman indicates in *When Parents Hurt*, "You can do everything right, and your child can still grow up and not want to have the kind of relationship with you that you always hoped for (3). Almost any reason to abandon a parent is used by the adult children, which is something the estranged cannot be responsible for.

Parents are not responsible for the decisions adult children make. If an adult child decides that abandoning a parent is in their best interest, then there is nothing a parent can do about that. It is bad luck. As Dr. Coleman has indicated, sometimes abused children don't even think of abandoning their parents, but children who are treated like royalty find abandoning them to be just fine. It is difficult to see the logic in that, especially when this action also means removing a grandparent from the grandchildren. It is emotional abuse of the children, especially if that grandparent had a good relationship with them.

Parents cannot punish themselves for the excessive behavior of their adult child, especially someone who does not know themselves well enough to recognize their behavior. The parent who may have thought they were responsible for the adult child's behavior, who feels guilt and regret for lousy parenting, must realize that the child's natural behavior is a genetic predisposition. In some respects, the lack of compassion and empathy is an unlearned behavior, but it can be part of the genetic makeup. If one is a narcissist, feeling compassion and empathy for someone is not in their character. It is unfortunate that one possesses that characteristic whether genetic or a learned behavior. Indifferent adult children simply do not care about the suffering of a grandparent who misses their grandchildren like nothing before. They are indifferent to the suffering of the parents and lack empathy and compassion. The Dali Lama said, "A person meditating on compassion for others becomes the first beneficiary." Perhaps there should be some more meditation on compassion.

When Joshua Coleman indicated that "some kids make their mediocre parents look and feel pretty great while others make their exceptional parents look and feel pretty awful." Perhaps that is all that this generation needs to give up on parents and grandparents. Perhaps, in their eyes, this was all justified behavior. Undoubtedly, this is done for reasons they believe are valid, if they could only be decent enough to express what those reasons are. Perhaps so, but I had a lot of physical and emotional hurt from my parents and never thought of banning them from my life or banning them from seeing my grandchildren. Sadly, it sometimes does not matter if one is a perfect parent and grandparent.

Another unfathomable reason parents cannot be responsible for their estrangement is that too much psychology is in the air. This generation may have read in *Psychology Magazine* or heard it on Dr. Phil says that ousting a parent is a good thing to do, ensuring they get rid of all those "toxic" people in their lives. Too many psychologists have used this term to refer to people that Millennials should discard, including their parents or grandparents. Dr. Coleman has written extensively about the wrong too many psychologists are doing by allowing their clients to oust their parents if the adult children consider their parents to be "toxic." Therapists have fostered more estrangements than any one group of people by labeling parents in this manner.

Perhaps the Millennials read somewhere that estranging a parent is okay to make them happy. It is their choice for whatever reason, and no one cannot change that. I do not consider this reason justifiable to cause so much pain and anguish. Their indifference to the pain and suffering of the parent or grandparent tells of their character and another reason why parents cannot accept responsibility for this happening.

Parents are also not responsible for the behavior their children learn from their peers. Peer pressure is often a difficult challenge for parents when a child decides that his peers are more important than his parents. Disagreements ensue, and parents are cast off as a result. Since ousting parents is a significant trend with this generation, it is more likely to happen because it has been "sanctioned" by other friends who have already made the move and ousted the parent(s). In other words, it must be okay if their friends are doing it. Peers influence their peers to behaviors that otherwise might not happen. There were challenges of peer pressure that we had as parents.

While parents can do all that they feel is best to bring up the children as best they can, other factors drive the child's behavior outside of the parent's influence. I remember finding some alcohol that we did not buy in the house after a party the kids had when we went away and trusted them. Of course, when we left for a short trip, our house became a haven for a teenage party, and kids who were not welcome were trying to get into the house. The outside flowers were trampled as people tried to enter the house through the windows. Finding out about this secret party disappointed my ex-wife and me, but fortunately, no significant damage was done to the house. I remember talking to my son about drinking hard liquor at his age and that I disapproved of his doing so. He just looked at me like I was an idiot and said nothing, his usual response to being criticized. But he was in a rebellious period and changing faster than I knew. I just gave the reader an example: peer pressure to "party" with booze in high school is more powerful than parents telling their children not to do such a thing. We trusted our children not to do something like that, but peer pressure overwhelmed our parental teachings. They went ahead and had the booze party anyway. We, as parents, had indeed indicated that drinking alcohol in high school is wrong. We strongly disagreed with doing something like that since I personally never drank alcohol when I was in high school (my parents would have killed me), and neither did my ex-wife. So peer pressure is beyond their control for even the best of parents.

Another peer pressure incident happened to my son when he was a junior: he had his hair dyed by his friends to blond. He was a brown-haired kid. My reaction was disgusted because it showed a "radical" departure from being a straight-laced kid. I told my son that he better cover his head well whenever the coach from Stanford came around because I did not want the coach to think my son was radical. Also, it was just before he was offered a scholarship to Stanford to play golf, but his buddies talked him into dying his hair. I could not change what he had done but warned him that such a move could jeopardize his chances for the scholarship. That spring, my son broke Tiger Woods's scoring record for the Southern California high school championships by shooting a 65 in the final round. He had won the high school championship of 583 high schools in Southern California for the second time. The coach of Stanford was so impressed that he ignored my son's hair rebellion and offered the scholarship that summer, only to rescind it a month later for no apparent reason. While I never learned why the coach did that, I worked on begging the coach to reinstate his scholarship, which he did reluctantly. Perhaps the coach saw a side of my son that even I was unaware of—a rebellious nature, a go-it-alone, and do-my-own-thing behavior.

Again, my son rebelled and did things I did not care for without knowing what was happening. He started going to hard rock concerts with a mosh pit, where he jumped in the fray and banged around his body. If he had injured himself enough not to play for the high school championship, his dream of getting the Stanford scholarship would have been over. Thankfully, nothing happened. On another occasion, he wanted to go snowboarding with friends. I did not permit it before his junior year golf championship because I was afraid he would hurt his hands falling on a snowboard he had never been on before. I was glad I kept saying no to him because he begged me to allow him to do it about five times. I finally had to be emphatic about it and tell him no means no. This shows how peer pressure is so great, and the need to "fit in" is more powerful than the rational thinking of the parent. Joshua Coleman indicates this in the quote: "Parents are not fully responsible for the children's behavior no matter what their training has been at home."

My ex-wife and I were in high school in the 1960s, and our music choice was the Beatles, the Stones, and the bands of that era. While they were considered "radical" for the period, the Beatles dressed in suits and ties. They were a formal group and looked conservative except for their hair; their music was conservative, all about love, friendship, and tame subjects. In the 1990s, my son, by comparison, was listening to Rage Against the Machine, a group that tells young people to tell authority to get lost. They were radical by comparison. I was so clueless that I did not know he was involved with crap groups like that, but I became aware of it at an important time. Whether his peers influenced him to listen to or pick them out was his choice.

More importantly, the child's culture may not be as influenced by parents as one thought. "Anthropologist Margaret Mead wrote that culture is 'the systemic body of learned behavior which is transmitted from parents to children.' While this sounds reasonable, we now recognize that parents are only one of the many ways children assimilate cultural values. In older children, peers seem to have a far more powerful effect than parents in transmitting culture" (Coleman 68).

Boomer parents felt it was essential to give a better life to their children than they had growing up. The shift in the family dynamics resulted from thinking that "hovering" over the child's every need was making life "better" for them when it put the parent too much in front of the child. In short, the children get too much of the parents. Boomer parents also felt that protecting children from failure was ensuring a better life for them when it was a total mistake. Children grow up without the ability to successfully deal with problems. Instead of working out a disagreement with a parent, it is easier for the adult child to eliminate them from their lives. Boomer parents had a different paradigm while growing up. Parents did their own thing, and kids found each other on the streets after school and played "kick the can" and "hide and seek." Parents were less involved with their children even though the mother was usually a stay-at-home mom and the father was the breadwinner.

For all these reasons, parents should not feel responsible for their estrangement. When a generation of young people jump on the bandwagon of abandoning their parents, it is a social phenomenon, not the derelict behavior of parents. It isn't justified, it isn't ethical, and it isn't moral. Parents can only do so much when rearing a child; the other contender is genetics. If a child is stubborn, violent, or unreasonable, then no amount of influence can alter that behavior. If there is a family history of this behavior, nothing can change that predisposition. For all of this happening at this time, there is a confluence of reasons why this estrangement phenomenon is happening.

Chapter 10, the role of narcissism in the creation of estrangements in America. How can estranged people take solace in the fact that estrangements are happening because a generation of young people think they are more critical than their parents?

CHAPTER 10:

The Role of Narcissism in Creating Estrangements

E stranged people can take solace in the fact that there are forces at work that have brought about this social phenomenon of estrangement. The generations that followed the Baby Boom Generation (1946-1964) were Generation X (1965-1980), Generation Y (1981-1996), and Generation Z (1997-2012). It is important to note that estrangement has escalated in each generation following the Boomer Generation. It is important as well to understand that each generation has a different set of values and that these values affect their decisions about their lifestyle, as was discussed in Chapter 11. For this chapter, I have reserved comments about the Millennial Generation because they have done the most estranging of their parents and grandparents. I will argue that this behavior has come about as a result in the rise in narcissism.

Since I devoted my life to serving the needs of my students as an English teacher for thirty-seven years, it is pretty hard to accept the criticism that I was a narcissist and that it was "looked up" and there was "evidence of it going back twenty years." Imagine someone diagnosing a father by "looking it up" online. It did not take me long to write back a response to this indictment of my fatherhood that was all for myself. It was pretty disturbing to learn that this perception of me as a father was that I did everything for myself during my fatherhood. Josh Coleman has indicated in *When Parents*

Hurt: Compassionate Strategies When You and Your Grown Child Don't Get Along that "part of what makes being a parent confusing is that our adolescent or adult children may accuse us of doing things that we didn't do; they may take our behavior completely out of context or may interpret behaviors that were intended to be loving and protective as selfish, hurtful, or ruinous." (Coleman 35). Nothing can be further than the truth. It matters what my child's version of my parenthood is when it differs from what happened. It is hard to imagine how one can draw that conclusion. I address what my ex-wife and I did to make a good life for our children in Section III. I don't think she or I accept this evaluation of our parenthood.

When I was accused of being selfish, it sent a dagger through my heart. I sent a letter to defend myself. I considered the short letter of attack on my character to be nothing but a projection of what the writer is—someone who grew up with all the privileges of the upper middle class. After a good deal of research and watching a president who has been identified as a sociopathic narcissist, I am pretty sure that the characteristics of narcissism have not ever reached my realm of life but that the Millennial Generation, of which the accuser is a part, has been characterized as a narcissistic generation. According to psychologist Claudia Sinay Mosias, "Narcissism is characterized by a grandiose sense of self-importance, a lack of personal empathy for others and a belief that one is special and deserving of special attention, and is exempt from normal rules, norms, and mores." (Medium.com) This is more likely to fit the accused's description than the accused's. Note that there is a lack of empathy, clearly demonstrated in the behavior of the estranger.

Joel Stein's article "The Me Me Me Generation" in *Time Magazine* gives a lot of faith to the idea. According to him, here are the cold, hard facts: "The incidence of narcissistic personality disorder is nearly three times as high for people in their 20s as for the generation that's now 65 or older, according to the National Institutes of Health, 58% more college students scored higher on a narcissism scale in 2009 than in 1982. Millennials got so many participation trophies growing up that a recent study showed that 40% believe they should be promoted every two years, regardless of performance. Millennials are fame-obsessed: three times as many middle school girls want to grow up to be a personal assistant to a famous person as want to be a Senator, according to a 2007 survey; four times as many would pick the personal assistant job over CEO of a major corporation. They're so convinced of their greatness that the National Study of Youth and Religion found the guiding morality of 60% of Millennials in any situation is that they'll just be able to feel what's right. Their development is stunted: more people ages 18 to 29 live with their parents than with a spouse, according to the 2012 Clark University Poll of Emerging Adults. And they are lazy. In 1992, the nonprofit Families and Work Institute reported that 80% of people under 23 wanted to one day have a job with greater responsibility; 10 years later, only 60% did.

In the scholarly article "The Narcissistic Millennial Generation: A Study of Personality Traits and Online Behavior on Facebook" by Julia Brailovskaia and Hans-Werner Bierhof, published online on November 23, 2018, we learn that the study aimed to investigate differences between later-born Millennials (1991-2000) and early born Millennials (1977-1990). The study looked at the personality trait of narcissism, sensation seeking, self-esteem, and Facebook use. They also investigated the relationship between personality traits and Facebook use in both groups. The study showed that the "Results of regression discontinuity analysis including age as covariate indicate that late Millennials, on average, score significantly higher on narcissism, sensation seeking, self-presentation, and social interaction on Facebook than early Millennials."

"In both groups, narcissism, sensation seeking, self-esteem, and online behavior were positively related. Interpretation of the results focuses on technological innovation and cultural change, which affect the development of early and late Millennials differently. It was concluded that late and early Millennials differ substantially regarding personality traits and online behavior. Recent research shows that the online behavior of the Millennial Generation differs considerably from older generations (Djamasbi et al. 2010; Hayes et al. 2015; Windisch and Medman 2008). Millennials, who are also called Net Generation or Generation Y, are the last-born generation of the twentieth century (born: 1977/80–2000; Tapscott 2009). Howe and Strauss (2003) defined the members of this generation "as special, sheltered, confident, team-oriented, conventional, pressured, and achieving. They are generally well educated, optimistic, and believe they can achieve everything they want." Parents, teachers, and others from their social network support them in reaching their goals (Tapscott 2009).

Twenge (2012; see also Twenge and Campbell 2009) described Millennials as entitled, self-centered, and narcissistic. In a cross-temporal meta-analysis of narcissism investigating American college students, results indicate that their level of open narcissism increased continuously across generations. Consequently, Generation Y had the highest narcissism scores compared to earlier generations (Twenge et al. 2008). In addition, personality traits related to narcissism (e.g., extraversion self-esteem) followed the same trend.

Narcissistic characteristics can be put on a spectrum with the full-blown narcissist with narcissistic personality disorder, someone like Donald Trump, who has every narcissistic characteristic known to man. At the same time, most people exhibit a modicum of traits. Some people are narcissistic, and then there is Narcissistic Personality Disorder, a full-blown narcissist. When one claims that an individual is narcissistic, they think it covers NPD but does not. The NPD is a person who has "a grandiose sense of self-importance, or a need for excessive admiration, a preoccupation with fantasies of unlimited success or rage in response to criticism. Narcissists also tend to be arrogant, lack empathy, and envy others." (Sinay-Mosias 1). It is the lack of empathy that sticks out in my mind. It is something I have experienced as a result of being estranged. Regardless of any appeal to reconciliation, there is no regard for the feelings of loss for the parent and grandparent.

These are the typical characteristics of a narcissist, with my comments in parentheses.

1. The conversation is always about you. (We all know someone like this.)
2. They feel uncomfortable focusing on others. (Especially when talking to their own parents and asking them how they are doing!)
3. They feel people love them. (Perhaps too much of it gives people this grandiose perception of themselves).
4. They expect others to put their needs before their own.
5. They are always right—many narcissists have to be right. (It is difficult for some people to admit they are wrong and take responsibility for being so.)

6. They can do no wrong. (Well, in their eyes they can do no wrong but in others, they are wrong.)

7. They are materialistic. (They think material things are more important than good relationships with family.)

8. They can't take criticism, just like they cannot face adversity. (That is for sure, given that any criticism leads to abandonment.)

9. They think they are truly special. (How else are they going to feel if this was said and told them while growing up? Parents did not want kids to have fragile egos, so they told them how special they were and averted failure.)

10. They need to be more successful than the people around them. (I am sure that their jobs are attached to their egos).

11. They will take advantage of others. (It is a trait of the narcissist.)

12. They think the rules don't apply to them. (If they make a mistake, they will not accept responsibility.)

13. They don't feel empathy for others. (Disregarding the feelings of the grandparents has demonstrated this problem. It does not matter what they do to a grandparent because they have zero compassion and zero empathy, both characteristics of narcissism)

14. They want everything perfect all of the time. (That can't happen)

15. They are obsessed with their appearance. (They will inform you if they don't care how someone else appears).

16. They feel a sense of entitlement. (If this isn't true of the Millennial generation, nothing is. Worse than that is the lack of gratitude.)

While most people do not exhibit all these characteristics, the full-blown narcissist has several behavioral issues. Beneath the seeming strong person is someone with vulnerability, shame, insecurity, and low self-worth—narcissism results from parents who doled out excessive adoration or criticism. The outcome is someone who tries to put themselves on a pedestal. Men are more likely to be narcissistic than women. The Millennial generation was just a group placed on a pedestal and told they could do no wrong. They are the result of excessive adoration.

The worst outcome of telling them this fable was fostering a generation of narcissists and the consequent estrangement epidemic we have in American society. Although one may disagree the two are connected, the fact that we have such a rise in individualism in this country is testimony to the expendability of the parents and grandparents for their happiness. There is a huge connection between a narcissistic generation and estrangement. As I have pointed out, this is a social phenomenon and not the issue of one single parent. But this social phenomenon has been fostered by the excessive adoration of a generation of entitled brats. While there is a difference between narcissism and narcissistic personality disorder, it is essential to understand that this generation has been deemed narcissistic through research on their generation. They toss about the word because they have learned it from television and other media sources without knowing the particulars of the behavior.

People who toss around terminology like "You're a Narcissist" are practicing what is called projection. Projection is calling someone else a quality that they possess. Projection is a defense mechanism by which an individual unconsciously attributes their behaviors, emotions, impulses, undesirable characteristics, and thoughts to others. It is a way of taking our internal dialogue and turning it into an external exchange, as if our beliefs or behaviors belong to someone else. Trump used to do this all the time, and every time he called out someone's shortcomings, he was talking about himself.

There are many causes of an empathy deficit. They include but are not limited to:

- A personality disorder: Some people who struggle to empathize with others may have a personality disorder that inhibits their ability to connect or communicate. Common personality disorders include narcissistic personality disorder (NPD), antisocial personality disorder, and borderline personality disorder (BPD).

- Autism spectrum disorder: Individuals on the autism spectrum may experience different levels of empathy, interpersonal skills, and emotional intelligence.

- Lack of awareness: Many people who lack empathy simply don't realize it and, therefore, haven't spent time and energy working to develop empathy.
- Self-awareness is a key step toward empathy.
- Lack of role models: Many unempathetic people have not had strong role models for empathetic behavior in their lives—or have had many models of unempathetic behavior instead.

Studies have shown that the Millennial Generation has the moniker of being a narcissistic group of people. Their self-serving behavior can lead to estranging a parent. In a study published in the *Journal of Adult Development* on November 23, 2018, Julia Brailovskaia and Hans-Wermer Bierhoff's work "The Narcissistic Millennial Generation: A Study of Personality Traits and Online Behavior on Facebook" relates well to what Dr. Coleman is saying about individualism in America. The author concludes that "Millennials, also called Net Generation or Generation Y, are the last born generation of the twentieth century (born 1977/1980-2000; Tapscott 2009). Howe and Strauss (2003) defined the members of this generation as special, sheltered, confident, team-oriented, conventional, pressured, and achieving. They are generally well-educated and optimistic and believe they can achieve everything they want. Parents, teachers, and others from their social network support them in reaching their goals (Tapscott 2009). However, besides this positive depiction, Twenge (2012; see also Twenge and Campbell 2009) described Millennials as entitled, self-centered, and narcissistic. The study indicates that "In a cross-temporal meta-analysis of narcissism investigating American college students, results indicate that their level of open narcissism increased continuously across generations."

Consequently, Generation Y, or the Millennials, reached the highest narcissism score compared with earlier generations (Twenge et al. 2008). In addition, personality traits related to narcissism (e.g., extraversion and self-esteem) followed the same trend (Campbell et al. 2002; Twenge 2001; Twenge and Campbell 2001). This study supports this generation's desire to value individualism over filial responsibility. In other words, they are more into themselves than they are into mending a relationship with a parent or grandparent.

Chapter 11 will discuss the conclusions about the estranged that I have drawn from my experience. These are the observations I made due to my unfortunate estrangement.

CHAPTER 11:

Conclusions I Have Drawn about the Estranged

Those who become estranged often have a multitude of questions as to why they have found themselves in this situation. There are several things that an estranged person must learn to understand themselves better as an estranged individual. Here are those things the estranged needs to understand and take action to learn.

ON TAKING RESPONSIBILITY

The first thing to realize is that this is a shared responsibility. That is, even though the parent may not feel responsible for the estrangement, there is something that they have done that has fostered it, whether the perception is right or wrong. They must listen to what Coleman says, which is that "kernel of truth" about them that must be understood. Many parents who suffer this fate find that compromising such behavior allows the adult child to take control of the situation. As I have indicated by the title of my book, this is precisely what is going on. They are taking control and "being the parent," many parents just don't find that acceptable. It is an upside-down world, and many parents don't want to participate. Most of the time, there is no reconciliation with adult children when parents don't want to downgrade themselves by allowing the adult children to take control. They are in control, and accepting responsibility for one's part in the disagreement is necessary for reconciliation. That is if one wants that to happen.

ON LEARNING SELF-COMPASSION

Self-compassion is the ability to forgive oneself for the mistakes one has made with one's family. Dr. Coleman stated more clearly, "Self-compassion is the ability to believe that, no matter how terrible your mistakes, love and forgiveness are part of your birthright and humanity. While your children do not owe you love and forgiveness, you should see compassion and forgiveness from other family members (if they're capable), your friends, a counselor, your faith, and yourself." (Coleman 31). The important thing I learned here is that my children do not owe me either love or forgiveness. Since they do not owe it to me, I have to give it to myself despite my apologies. That is what self-compassion is. I learned that although I did not get compassion or love from my children, I got it from friends, siblings, and family members who were sympathetic to my fate. They helped me deal with the rejection.

I have sought solace from several family members and friends, and they have been incredibly supportive. My friends and family cannot believe that forgiveness is not a part of the makeup of some people. However, the reason(s) for our estrangement remain unknown, making the practice all the more cruel.

ON SHAME

Shame is a consequence of being estranged, and a parent needs to understand that this emotion will take over one's life when one becomes estranged. As I have already indicated earlier in the book, Brene Brown defines shame as: "It's that feeling that washes over you, that makes you feel like you're small and you're not good enough, and that you're not worthy of love and connection with your friends and your family." Much of what a parent feels as a result of estrangement is shame. It's a shame they have this kind of relationship with their family. It is a shame that they cannot discuss what their family is doing because they don't know. It is a shame because one is treated as if one does not matter. It's like I have no use for the family and have been discarded like a used tissue. Shame attacks the ego and humiliates someone, and one's sense of self-worth diminishes. Thoughts of worthlessness and suicidal thoughts come from the shame felt from being abandoned. It makes the person think they are a bad parent, and it makes someone feel bad about themselves.

As Josh Coleman indicates in *When Parents Hurt: Compassionate Strategies When You and Your Grown Child Don't Get Along*, "parenting becomes more treacherous as children grow because their capacity to reject, shame, and humiliate the parent increases in weight and power as they get older" (81). In his book *Rules of Estrangement: Why Adult Children Cut Ties and How to Heal the Conflict*, Dr. Coleman states, "Every time I am interviewed in national media, I am besieged with referrals and emails from estranged parents who all say the same thing: 'I thought I was the only one!' Parents don't talk about estrangement to their friends, co-workers, or even their own family because they fear judgment. They fear someone will say or think: 'What did you do to your child? It must have been something terrible" (Coleman 1). Indeed, the power to humiliate and shame are the pathetic behaviors used by the adult children, and that is why they "jangle the keys of the kingdom" when they feel like it.

ON THE LOSS OF REPUTATION

Along with suffering from shame, one of the dire effects of abandonment is damaging the reputation of the ostracized parent. Shakespeare makes poignant comments about reputation in the play *Othello*. "But he that filches from me my good name robs me of that which does not enrich him and makes me poor indeed" (Iago 3.3.159–61). Both Cassio and Iago struggle with losing their reputation. It is indeed central to one's estrangement. Imagine explaining estrangement to someone who does not even know what it means. It is a terrible consequence for the estranged parent. Does it matter to anyone?

Try to put yourself into the parent's shoes, or as Atticus Finch says in *To Kill a Mockingbird*, "You never really understand a person until you consider things from his point of view... until you climb in his skin and walk around in it." (Lee 39). Imagine a person asking if you have any children, and you answer, "Yes, but I have not talked to them for several years, nor have I seen my grandchildren." The immediate reaction of the person hearing this is to say they are sorry, and they do not pursue it any further. But this happens in their minds: "What did **HE** do wrong to deserve such a fate?" Undoubtedly, any person's reputation is diminished by the knowledge that they are estranged from their children. The parent is automatically blamed. Rightfully so, but it takes more than the parent to make this happen.

I told my story to this mortgage banker, and his response was, "Oh, my, there is nothing more important than family." I told him I agreed, which was the end of our conversation. It was gratifying to learn that at least some Millennials value family and do not toss them out the window like used garbage. Losing one's reputation as a parent became the **Scarlet Letter** I had to wear. It is particularly disconcerting to have to live with that label. Not only does one become a designated witch, but one who has that moniker on them throughout their lives. As Iago in Shakespeare's *Othello* says, "Reputation is an idle and most false imposition, oft got without merit and lost without deserving." (Iago 2.4.268–70) I simply do not deserve to have this Albatross hanging around my neck. It has been a burden for a long time, and it weighs heavily. It weighs heavily on my reputation as a parent. It is undeserved. That, of course, is my view.

If I had been a terrible father or a terrible Grandfather, I could understand being rejected, but I was neither of those. Who throws their parents under the bus? Indeed, those who do such a thing lack compassion, the ability to forgive, and a fundamental respect for the parent. All estranged parents who have not violated egregious acts against their children don't deserve such treatment.

ON COMMUNICATION

The worst thing I experienced with the Millennial children was their inability to communicate regularly. With the geographic differences between us, it takes an effort to pick up the phone and call the parents. This is the hallmark of the problem with families today. Kids get their jobs in different states, and communication becomes more challenging. The less one communicates the more wary one becomes of the other. This is one of the failings of the current generation. They lack a desire to call their parents and communicate with them. Calling a parent is only essential if it is about them.

I always called my parents in my 20s, 30s, 40s, and 50s. I called them until the day they died. I was a busy guy all during that time, but somehow,

I found the time to call them. When I called my parents, I asked them what they were up to. I asked them how they were doing. I asked them if they needed any help. I made a lot of effort to help and stay in touch with my parents for my entire married life. At the end of their lives, I did not want to think they had not heard from me. Some of the six kids in my family kept a good line of communication with my mother and father, and none would say they were "great parents." I am sure it can be said they were below average. Yet, it did not deter our respect for them. We grew up with the understanding to honor our father and our mother. And we did. And we regularly communicated with them.

Honoring and respecting them was done even though my parents were physically and emotionally abusive. They did not hesitate to take out the belt and deliver whacks on our backside for doing practically nothing. Even though there was resentment for that treatment, we forgave them for their mistakes and accepted them for who they were as adults. We still loved them despite their old-fashioned quirks. Looking away from errors made by parents is not a value or behavior of the Millennial generation, and their generation seems to be willing to throw the parents under the bus for even the slightest misbehavior on the part of the parents. That is why our society has an epidemic of parents being tossed under the bus by the Millennial generation. They don't value their parents; they value themselves and what is best for their happiness. Throw the parents under the bus if they don't fit their happiness role. Or do they just value those parents who will give them a legacy? This is important because they value material things more than family.

The most aggravating aspect of this "shunning" is not giving a reason for doing such a thing. Are they incapable of communicating? On this account, this is where we, as parents, failed. The ability to communicate is pathetic. Are there reasons for not wanting to communicate? Did they just decide, like a great preponderance of their fellow Millennials, that they don't need to justify the shunning? If an adult child wants to sever ties with a parent, the least they can do is tell them why they are doing it! It goes to the problem of the inability to communicate. Are they afraid to communicate, or are they afraid to tell their side of the story or hear my side of the story and how they hurt me immeasurably for taking away the grandchildren? Their decision not to communicate a reason for shunning a parent constitutes elder abuse, the conclusion of the most prominent estrangement expert here in the United States. Elder abuse! I am sure they are just fine (a sarcastic term that Hemingway used in his novels) with this.

How would children feel if their parents ignored all their requests for help in high school and college? How would they feel if they just ignored their requests and did not tell them why they were ignoring them? I imagine they would have been mad about that. It is cruel and unjustified not to say why they are doing this. It speaks volumes about their character. It adds to the punishment of being banned, ostracized, abandoned, or estranged, whichever term suits one's fancy.

One of their aunts said that they always kept lines of communication open in their family, preventing many problems. I thought communication was a problem when I talked to their mother, who indicated she received fewer phone calls (mostly because techy Millennials like to text) from the adult children than she expected. She would not complain about something like that for fear of retribution from them.

Another area for improvement with what they value is that communication could have been higher on their list. Most of the time, it was through a phone text comment if they were communicating. A lot of times, it was one word! Their inability to communicate broke down any closeness we had established as parents. The less they communicated, the more distant they became from their parents. Their lifestyle is more important than their extended family. I just don't see how anyone cannot learn basic human decency. Their inability and unwillingness to communicate is a step to breaking down the fabric of the American family.

ON LOVE

When I came home at night after teaching at the college, I always visited my kid's rooms to pat them good night and tell them I loved them even when they were already asleep. Such a treatment was missing from my mother and father when I was a child, and I would be sure my kids did not have the same fate. When my father went to California, he hugged each of the kids, but it was not what one would call a warm one. Hugging the kids before bedtime and telling them I loved them all the time when the kids were children was a constant in our house. I do not doubt loving my children during their entire upbringing. The things I did were for the entire family, and how they were raised was successfully verified by the letter a friend of my daughter wrote to her on the day of her marriage. I do not have the letter, but it was an explicit endorsement of the beautiful upbringing my wife and I had with our children.

My mother and father never hugged us at night before sleeping. They just proclaim, "Get to Bed!" Off we went to take care of our preparations for bedtime. No one read books to me every night so that I could have the advantage of being able to read when I arrived in kindergarten. I had to catch up with my reading when I was going to school and spend hours and hours reading books to improve my language and writing ability. I wrote in a journal for ten years to help improve my writing. I wrote and wrote to improve my ability to communicate on paper. I did not have the early advantages my children had.

There was not enough "I love you," said in our family, and perhaps that is why one can easily toss away a parent. Most families have quarrels and feuds but do not toss their parents out the window when troubles arise. Parents that were abusive to their children don't have them throw the parents out the window when a disagreement occurs.

These are just some of the conclusions I have drawn from my estrangement. In the meantime, the crazy little children are jangling the keys of the kingdom. One day, those keys will be in the next generation's hands.

Chapter 12 will attempt to share what generational shift in values means and that what is prized by one generation is not prized by another. The next generation will supposedly do things better than the previous generation, but it appears America is going backward.

CHAPTER 12:

Generational Differences—A Shift in Family Values

The estranged need to realize that a shift in the values of the newer generations has brought about the explosion in estrangement. As each new generation succeeds the other, the newer generation seeks to adopt and reject the previous generation's values. As the reader learned in the first chapter, the estrangement problem is at epidemic proportions. This chapter will explore the Millennials' values that differ radically from previous generations. In an essay entitled "A Shift in American Family Values Is Fueling Estrangement," Coleman explains the change in American Society. "Where prior generations of children were expected to earn the parents' love and respect, today's parents are worried that they won't have their children's love and respect because they are not enough, not "there" enough. They're worried, often correctly, that their real or imagined mistakes in parenting may one day come back to haunt them" (73).

First, he claims that the mobility and dispersion of families have fostered less communication among family members. Geographic dispersion has fostered poor communication, and misunderstandings become common. This happened with my family; my daughter moved to Seattle, my son to Dublin, Ireland, and then Boulder, Colorado. Although I moved to Colorado to be near my son and grandchildren, we were over an hour and a half away in Colorado Springs. Still, communication was difficult because both my son and his wife worked, and there needed to be more effort to keep in touch. My son's family took up skiing, distancing them even further. My daughter was also too busy teaching and raising her daughter, and communication dwindled as the years passed. This generation believed it was the parents responsibility to contact them, not their responsibility to contact the parents. If I did not hear from my children for months, I had to call them in order to see what they were doing.

Coleman also claims that in the past fifty years, all working parents have worked harder than ever to be good parents. Parents gave up their lives to work harder to improve their children's lives. He said they gave up hobbies, sleep, and time with friends and their spouses to help their offspring into successful adulthood. Parents went from disregarding their children during the Baby Boomer generation to becoming "helicopter" parents of the Millennial generation. Boomer parents moved away from their own lives and "lived" the lives of their children, something that helped foster the estrangement problem. This is why Boomer parents have been accused of living through their children when the reality was they were just trying to make life better for them than what they had experienced.

Brene Brown has indicated that the correct paradigm for a strong family is for the parents to stay close and bonded to each other instead of surrendering their role to the importance of the child's life. She said placing the children on a pedestal and catering to them in helicopter parent fashion is a recipe for disaster. In my case, this became quite true. My ex-wife and I catered to the growth of our children and lost each other in the process. When we became empty-nesters, there was nothing that we had in common because we had not developed those commonalities over the years that would serve us to be together in our retirement years. We divorced just after my son finished college.

Millennials did not learn to value family except their own. Their lives and their family are more important than the extended family. They demonstrate no interest in other family members. My children chose not to engage my brothers and sisters nor their mother's brother on her side. On the other hand, baby boomers value total family get-togethers. This happened despite my family and my relationship with my parents despite the harsh discipline I received from them. My children needed a relationship with their grandparents, and every opportunity we had was to see that my parents participated in family get-togethers. We had Thanksgiving at our house for many years, and the entire family was invited to the gathering. My parents would come to the house for Mother's Day and Father's Day dinner, or we would take them to dinner. It was their special day. We included them at Christmas and Easter as well when they were available. We did that because that is what families traditionally do.

Once in Colorado, my wife called my son and asked him what they were doing for New Year's Eve. My daughter was already there with her family at my son's house, but there was no intent on us being a part of that get-together. Rather than saying no to my wife, my son invited us to come to the house for that holiday. But he and my daughter were not planning to have us come until my wife took the chance and called them. This demonstrates why neither of them value extended family and that they would have been fine with just each other.

Another generational difference is that the Millennials do not value family history. Whenever I ever talked about or shared information about the family history, I always felt my children could care less about it. Most of the time, they did not even ask questions about it. Learning about the origins of one's family on their father's side is fundamental to knowing who they are. I don't think they have a clue about who they think they are, but it does not matter to them. Filial responsibility is not a value they possess, so why would learning about family background matter? I think that they have no interest in family history or ancestors. It just isn't essential to them. They do not value it.

Also, they do not value their parents because what is important to them is what they want to talk about rather than what the parents may want to talk about. My conversations with my ex-wife during this crisis taught me that my children do not have time to call her as often as she would have liked. A phone call from either after my two operations, asking how I was doing, would have been much appreciated. Did they call their mother and ask how that hip replacement is going? A fundamental value of any generation is to be kind enough to call the parents and ask how they are doing. It isn't as if communication devices aren't available no matter where one lives in this country—calling either of us as parents happens without regularity. They were busy doing their own thing, too into themselves.

When they did have time to call home, It was always about what they were up to or what problem they were experiencing. My daughter would say, this guy said that, another guy said this, my principal is stupid, my boss is a jerk, and on and on about her life's problems. When I visited my son in Ireland, it was all about his issues and his concern about working and living in Ireland. I never heard, "How are you doing since your operation, Dad?" Their conversations were about their lives and not about their parent's lives. I found that they valued everything about their lives, not mine.

The current generation does not value grandparents. There is no need for older people in adult children's lives because they do not value their contributions to their grandchildren's development. If a grandparent is expendable, then there is no value in that grandparent. This generation does not see the importance of those older family members to their children's development. It has been established in the last chapter.

The Millennial generation values money and material things like their parents, but many have been hindered by the college debt they had to incur. If one managed to get through school with all college debt paid, they should appreciate those parents who worked and planned for that to happen. For some reason, they felt they were entitled to it. It is a value I did not ever want to have, given that my college education was paid for entirely by myself. They are happiest making money for their pleasure. The number of vacations my kids have taken far exceeds anything I ever experienced. The only cure for entitlement is learning gratitude.

There is no question about a shift in family values from my generation to the Millennials. Their family is most important, and the extended family is expendable. If there is a grandparent they deem intrusive, they throw them under the bus as fast as possible. Older people are just not valued, and I cannot tell the reader how many older people in my community live lonely lives because their children do not have time for them. Our community reminds me of the Beatle's song, "Eleanor Rigby," where all the lonely people sit and wait for the end of their lives. At the same time, those in this community are waiting for a phone call from their kids, and it never comes. I have met tons of them.

In chapter thirteen, it is important to know the stages of estrangement, which are pretty similar to the stages of grief. The estranged can benefit from this knowledge to understand what they are going through.

CHAPTER 13:

Why Knowing the Stages of Estrangement and Stages of Grief are Important and Other Research

I t is essential to know that the estranged go through stages of grief because they have lost their family. Since this is new territory for the estranged person, they may not know they are going through something similar to the grieving process. The stages of the grieving process (denial, anger, bargaining, depression, and acceptance) are the process one goes through after the loss of someone they love. Both of these stages of grief are comparable but slightly different in definition. I am not going to compare them but wanted the reader to know that this is essentially what one is going through when they become estranged from a loved one in the family. Each of the stages is fluid, meaning that one can bounce from one to another without actually realizing that is what is happening. To be aware that an estranged person is going through this is the important purpose of this chapter.

The stages of the estrangement process are different from the stages of grief but equally as traumatizing. The stages of estrangement are Shock, Despair, Acceptance, Transformation, and Maintenance. For the estrangement stages, it is common for people to bounce among them, skipping some while visiting others repeatedly. Some stages may be skipped, while others will repeatedly present themselves. For this narrative, it is essential to know what a parent can experience due to having their children abandon them or have their grandchildren taken from them.

The first stage is shock. The parent wants to know why this is happening. While the estranged parent is unaware of why the adult child is doing this to them, most parents say that they were not given a reason why the adult child is treating them like a harmful virus. The parent is at first unaware that this is happening because the adult child does not tell them there will be no more contact. The adult child just decides that they have had enough of the parent or grandparent and ceases contact. In my situation, my son and daughter-in-law made no notification that they did not want any future contact with me. After several months of no contact, I realized no contact would exist. Although my son sent me some "advice" for what I should be doing with my life, I did not regard it as the end of the road with them, but it was.

The second stage is Despair. Parents estranged from their adult child can spend much time in Despair. This is a difficult stage and one that is hard to tolerate. It will reappear several times during essential days in the lives of adult children and grandchildren. Tina Gilbertson, an LPC or Licensed Professional Counselor, says, "Feelings of powerlessness characterize the Despair stage." Since the adult child has grabbed the power by denying the parent any relationship with the family, the estranged feels completely powerless. When an adult child breaks ties with the parent, there is not much one can do. Even though I realized I was not being contacted, I continued to send gifts and notes to the grandchildren and Happy Father's Day to my son, but there was no response. The Despair became quite real. Gilbertson says, "Despair can be punctuated by anger, resentment, and even vengeful thought toward the rejecting child." When I realized there would be no contact, my wife became angry. I was also quite angry that my son and my daughter-in-law decided to cut ties with us. So, the estranged parent will find themselves in the throes of despair. It is an awful feeling. It lasts a long time and is not resolved until one gets help. Help can come from other family members from the clergy or a good psychologist. I will speak more about getting help in Chapter 16. Even though I found myself estranged, I was unaware that a parent or grandparent would be going through the stages of grief. I knew I was depressed about how I was being treated and was going through a wide range of emotions.

The third stage is Acceptance. As a parent, I had to accept things before I could change them. This is a stage where one must resign to the reality of the loss. Everyone who has had this happen must allow themselves to grieve over the loss and be mad about it. Crying about it and losing control is okay because this is the beginning of healing. Even though I had not accepted the situation, I continued to ask for forgiveness and apologized in every way I could. The frustration was not getting any response for my efforts for something that was not serious. The radical decision was still justified in the mind of my son. Only he can tell me why such a radical decision was made. I have had no response to my queries.

The fourth stage of estrangement is transformation. Again, according to Gilbertson, some parents realize that "their quality of life is better without the estranged child in it." Parents "consciously let go of attempts to reconcile and reshape their lives to suit the new reality." Parents learn to accept the new reality of their lost relationship with their adult children and grandchildren. This phase is when parents end their speculation about what caused the estrangement. In my situation, I have stopped communicating with them. Although there was an inadvertent contact, it was not a good one. My son is still angry, and I doubt if he will ever stop being so because of his genetic makeup. I have moved on and try not to trouble myself by thinking about something I have little control over. After all, I did not decide to end our relationship. As the reader knows, I turned to my writing as part of my therapy to deal with this tragedy. I am writing for myself and those going through the same issue.

The fifth stage is Maintenance. This stage is characterized by living daily with what feels like the new normal. If there is a reconciliation, then the relationship will have changed. It will never be the same. If there is no reconciliation, then that is the end, and let the adult child live with the decision. When I go to my grave, I can assure the reader I will not be thinking of those who abandoned me. I will let them resolve it by themselves. I have suggested what their fate may be.

Through the experience of being estranged, I have traversed through all of the stages described to the reader. Learning the different stages helped me understand what I was going through. Learning to live life without them is part of what acceptance is. I can get up every day and not be overwhelmed by it. Losing them never does leave the mind as it would not have they all died in an accident.

Chapter fourteen presents several important things an estranged person can do to help themselves. Learning self-compassion is of utmost importance and critical to the mental health of the estranged.

CHAPTER 14:

How Those Who are Estranged Can Help Themselves

I t would not be right to write this book without some advice to my fellow sufferers of estrangement. Although I am not an expert on handling this problem, I have some advice based on my experience. I want my readers to know that it is vital to do their best to understand their situation, and I hope that some of this book has done that for them. This book initially started as a letter to my children about my experience with estrangement, but it was very caustic and angry. Most of my readers would understand about getting angry when a child or adult tosses the parent out of their lives and the lives of their grandchildren. I am not sure which is worse: losing one's children or grandchildren. They are equally as painful. Here are a few suggestions for my readers about what they can do to help themselves.

Learning self-compassion is of utmost importance to good mental health. I have already addressed this in a previous chapter, but want to emphasize the importance of learning how to treat oneself well during this crisis. There are affirmations one can make to improve self-worth. These exercises are statements of affirmation one can make on a daily basis to allow the individual to improve their well being. Telling oneself that they are a good person who did not look for this situation and that it was not intentionally caused is a good start.

Although many of my readers are not writers, writing down your feelings in a log is essential. Take a notebook and a pen and have it handy whenever the time comes when you want to vent your anger or just write about the situation. It is how I began, and it helped me to see what I was dealing with. So, write what you feel and how you deal with losing contact with your loved ones. Write down what you did well as a father or mother, and write what you have accomplished as a person in your career.

Learn as much about estrangement as one can. Reading the book *When Parents Hurt: Compassionate Strategies When You and Your Adult Child Don't Get Along* by Josh Coleman is a good start. In it, the estranged will find many pearls of wisdom and a wonderfully supportive person who knows what it feels like to be estranged. He had suffered the same fate with his daughter from his first marriage, and so he knows what it is like because he has been there. Learn about the stages of estrangement so that you can recognize when you are going through one of them and when you might transition to another. These stages are fluid, and one may go back and forth. But knowing what they are and how they affect you is essential. It helps you to understand how you are feeling.

Read also those books and articles that offer suggestions for mending your relationship with your children. There are dozens of articles about this issue, and many offer suggestions for mending the relationship. Several books, including Josh Coleman's *Rules of Estrangement,* offer great suggestions on restoring normalcy in your relationships with your children. *Reconnecting with your Estranged Adult Child* by Tina Gilbertson is also an excellent treatment of suggestions to mend the relationship.

Seek solace from other members of your family or the clergy or support groups. You must talk to someone about your estrangement. They can offer a perspective that can help you deal with the problem. Many family members offered insights and support for my situation, and it was a relief to know that they understood how I was as a parent and supported me. It helped me deal with the pain and suffering a great deal, and I highly recommend engaging them with this issue. Also, a clergy member will be more than willing to advise on improving relations with the children and listening to your grieving. Some support groups share the same problem, and it is wonderful to connect with fellow sufferers of this situation.

It is highly recommended to stay in touch with your grandchildren to let them know that you still care about them despite being unable to see them.

They will one day be an adult, and if you happen to be around when they are, you may have that opportunity to speak to them and tell your side of the story. Staying in touch with them may make this easier.

It is important to stop blaming yourself for everything that has happened because none of it can be your fault entirely. One has to learn to practice self-compassion, being nice to yourself instead of punishing yourself. Look at the good side of things and see the glass as half full and not half empty. Try to be optimistic about the future instead of pessimistic about it.

Make yourself willing to forgive your child or children for doing this to you. It will take the burden of feeling solely responsible for your situation. Take to heart the comments about forgiveness and forgive yourself before forgiving others.

There are no doubt many other things that an estranged person can do that will be suggested by those who are authorities. As someone who knows what you are going through, I wish you all the best in finding peace with your family.

With these bits of wisdom, I leave the reader with another insight into estrangement: "For all of its glory and gut-busting work, parenting is a dangerous undertaking. You put in long hours, examine every decision and action, and do the best you can, and yet the child who once adored and needed you can come to reject, shame, and belittle you. The youth who was to be your greatest source of joy and pride can become your greatest source of worry and disappointment. The sweetest kid who wrote you love notes and gave hugs has written you off or gives you the finger instead." (Coleman 50)

CHAPTER 15:

The Dramatic Effects of Estrangement on the Family

E ven though a divorce breaks up a family, there is still contact between the family members. Estrangement is the complete loss of the family. The family one once knew no longer exists, is no longer a part of one's life, or has disappeared forever. It is not different than a complete loss by an airplane crash or some such horrific event.

A secondary consequence is a loss of trust. Trusting someone requires demonstrating their ability to say what they want in a controlled environment. When a family member loses the trust of another family member, it is difficult to restore. Estrangement causes the parents to lose trust in the adult child. It is vital to continuing a relationship, so it must be restored.

There is a general loss of respect for each other when something like this happens. People must look past the problem of not respecting the other side because they must realize their love for the other person. If they still love that other person, then respect for them can be reinstated.

There is the loss of time with the grandchildren and a general disappointment in being able to be part of their lives. One cannot cry over the loss of time but be happy if the time with the grandchildren is restored. All parties must move forward and cannot dwell on past mistakes, or there might not be a successful transition back to being together. This also applies to losing time with adult children that one cannot return. And the loss of celebrating the holidays, the birthdays, and the anniversaries as well.

In Part III of this book beginning with Chapter 16, I work to show how hard my ex-wife and I worked to provide an ideal childhood for our children. It is important to demonstrate how much effort we made as parents.

PART III:

WRITTEN IN DEFENSE OF OUR PARENTING AND MY GRANDPARENTING

How My Wife and I Worked Hard for the Success of Our Children

A psychologist told me that it is best to relate to the reader the kind of parenting my ex-wife and I did for our children. The purpose is to show that no egregious acts of raising our children ever occurred in our household. There was no abuse of any kind. There was nothing but a loving and idyllic childhood provided for those children. I want the reader to know what we did to provide that idyllic life and show that anyone can become a victim of estrangement, no matter how good or bad the parenting was. This chapter is a story about how we arrived at that idyllic location.

My ex-wife and I were two Baby boomers who grew up in the 1950s and 1960s. We both came from want and did everything possible to make life better for our children than we had experienced. Our children had an ideal upbringing in the 1980s and 1990s. (This, of course, is my version of ideal). A parent's view of our children's upbringing is far more accurate than the version the children will give the reader. If they wish to give their version, let them write their book. My argument will be that our parenting was outstanding by all accounts and measures.

My wife was born in Newburg, New York, but her family moved to California when she was just a child. First, it was the San Diego region of California before they settled in Orange, California. She was the oldest of two, and she had a brother who was three years younger. Their mother and father were not professionals, so they struggled financially during their childhood and teenage years. It would eventually drive the younger brother to seek fortune. It would be a driver for both children who wanted a better life than their parents could provide. During the teenage years, the mother and father divorced, and the mother became the sole provider for the children. She managed to get them to adulthood, and it was then that the two siblings made decent lives for themselves.

My wife worked hard in school, sometimes using her studies to distance herself from the emotional badgering that her mother did of her. She got excellent grades at Orange High School and earned a scholarship to Chapman University. She even took a trip to the University of Seven Seas, a floating college that Chapman sponsored for several years. Additionally, she went to Germany as an exchange student and excelled in learning the German language while she was there. She worked nights as a waitress to earn money to do these things and finished her degree and teaching credential in record time. She was immediately hired to teach in the Fountain Valley School District, where she would spend forty years of her life, primarily teaching third-grade students. She was considered an outstanding teacher and was praised for being so many times. She was dedicated to her work.

Despite the adverse conditions of her upbringing, she managed to make a promising career for herself. During these adverse times, people are often driven to accomplish things they never thought possible. She managed to do so despite the emotional badgering she took from her mother. Her mother was Columbian, and they tended to favor the boys in the family over the girls. Her mother was a strict disciplinarian, and my wife was often put on restriction for practically doing nothing. My wife grew up a child of the Baby Boom era. Parents were "old-fashioned" and strict. They took an authoritarian approach to parenting. A child did not speak until spoken to and would never contest the parent's decisions. It was simply unheard of. A child of that era followed the dictates of the parents, whether they were right or wrong. Children were to be grateful that they had a roof over their heads and food on the table.

My wife's family was impoverished. They did not have a telephone or carpet on the floor in their house. The father made a meager salary and was not considered very ambitious. The discord ended in divorce during the early years of the two children's teenhood. The mother then spent years shielding her children from the father despite his efforts to contact them. There were a lot of angry feelings from the mother about the father of her two children, and the bitterness led to an estrangement of the father from the children. It was only near his death that the son saw the father before he passed away. My wife never saw him after the divorce. Despite these adverse conditions when growing up, she never considered abandoning her mother.

I was born in the late 1940s in Canton, Ohio, to a father with an eighth-grade education and a mother who graduated from high school. I was the fifth of six children. My father struggled to provide for the family without an education, and we went without many times during our childhood. As a child, I was often hungry when I went to bed. Fortunately, my father got a job in California in the late 1950s, so we moved there after I had finished 6th grade. During our time in Ohio, we had moments when they were none too kind. When we misbehaved, we were whipped with a belt on our legs and backside. What constitutes child abuse today was not child abuse in those days. My father's father took the belt to the children of his family, and the "tradition" of using the belt carried on. I learned to resent authority and adults who mistreated anyone when I was young. When we got whipped, we cried a lot, tears that were real from the pain and suffering of being hit by a leather belt. My mother was also not a saint, often using a hanger to whack us when she saw fit. There were two girls and four boys, and the boys got the whippings, but the girls were spared. We all agreed that it was unfair. It was a harsh upbringing.

Arriving in California was fortunate, as we were the younger children. We went to good public schools and got a decent education. We managed to go to college for free, except for our book costs for the first two years of our education. When it came time to get that college education, it was all on us to do it since my parents could not afford anything in the way of support. So I got jobs, borrowed money, went through school, and got my secondary teaching credential to teach English at the high school level. I wanted to be a teacher because I thought that there would be time to live a good life if I did so. I never regretted my decision to teach. It was an excellent career.

Working for several years during college taught me the importance of resilience and confronting adversity. I was determined to get an education and live my life at a better level than my father was able to. And I did get my degree in English, a secondary teaching credential, a master's degree in English, and a master's in reading. I went to school for a long time and managed to pay for all of my expenses in school while paying for my own living space and car at the same time. It was challenging, but I managed to do it. Again, I experienced similar things that my future wife experienced: overcoming the difficulty of getting educated without parental support, overcoming the adversities of getting educated in colleges that demanded a great deal, and overcoming all the challenges of keeping a balanced life while pursuing an important goal.

After a few years of teaching, I purchased my first house in Fullerton, California, for thirty-three thousand dollars. I had a mortgage of two hundred and seventy-five dollars a month. My soon-to-be wife had a converted apartment into a condo as her living quarters. We announced our engagement in November of 1977, with a marriage date of June 24, 1978. In the meantime, we asked her brother to find us a house in Villa Park for under one hundred thousand dollars. Villa Park was one of the most exclusive cities in Orange County, and finding a house there for under 100 thousand was nearly impossible unless the people who lived in the property did not know the value of it. That fall, we managed to buy a house there for 84,500 dollars, but it took a lot of work to get it in livable condition. It took us several months to get the property cleaned and ready for move-in. This is the kind of hard work it took to get to our ultimate destiny: Irvine.

The work of redoing the house was complex and challenging. The entire house had to be gutted and redone. On one side of the property was a fifty feet long by fifteen feet wide driveway that went to the wrong side of the house. A garage needed to be built on the other side of the house, so I removed the driveway by breaking it up with sledgehammers and hauled the concrete to the dump. My next-door neighbor was so helpful with his truck because he was motivated to see our property improve. A garage was added to the house, and it looked beautiful when it was done. I remember the toil of digging trenches for a sprinkler system for our half-acre grass property. There were considerable tasks to overcome. However, by the fall of 1978, we were settled into our newly refurbished house and enjoying it for once.

Before long, a new opportunity came up. My ex-wife's brother and his partner built new houses with views of Orange County just a few miles from where we lived. We decided to sell the Villa Park house and move into a brand-new one a few miles away. We did so, but the work it took to put in the landscape was enormously challenging. When we sold our Villa Park house, it was on an AITD or All Inclusive Trust Deed. The buyer promised to pay us "X" for the house in two years. If he could not buy it for the agreed amount in two years, it would return to us. When the two years were up, he bought the house from us, and we had enough money to buy our dream home in Irvine. We managed to sell our house in Orange and broke even with the sale of that property, but we had a large amount of cash for the new house in Irvine from the proceeds of the Villa Park home. We packed up and went to a rental in Irvine to wait for the sale of the newly built homes we wanted to buy.

In the fall of 1984, we purchased a house in Irvine on a hill where the ocean was visible and the Hollywood sign was on a clear day. The view was from a hill in Irvine with a five-hundred-foot elevation. We moved into the house in April of 1985, and the children were four and six years old. We had accomplished our dream of raising children in one of the best neighborhoods in Irvine, or in Orange County, for that matter.

So we had accomplished what we had set out to do: live in a great neighborhood in Irvine that would provide a good education for the children. The elementary school was within walking distance, and the after-school care was situated down the street at a city park. The kids had after-school care, and they had great schools to attend. We provided them with the best that could be offered then. Both kids spent their entire schooling in the same area and grew up with many friends. The local high school was ranked highly academically and was an excellent foundation for college. Both of my kids found college easier than the high school they attended. It was academically rigorous.

I never once heard my children complain about their upbringing or childhood. The kids were six and four when we moved into our house at 2 Miranda in Irvine. When we bought the house, interest rates were 14%, and the mortgage would be challenging. Fortunately, the interest rates dropped to 10% when we closed on the house in April of 1985. We felt very fortunate to be able to buy this house, but we planned to give our children the best education we thought was available at the time. So we moved to the exclusive neighborhood of Turtle Rock in Irvine, where doctors, lawyers, dentists, and significant business people lived (like the company's CEO who built the house). Teachers did not buy houses like this, but my wife and I had put in a great deal of work on the homes we previously had to come up with a hundred thousand down on the new house. Our housing payment was still twenty-two hundred a month, and it was a struggle for several years before we refinanced the house and lowered the payment.

Before we got to Irvine, it was a long, hard road. It took great discipline to keep the house we had when we were there. We sacrificed a great deal: We never went out to eat, hardly took vacations in the first several years, and waited for interest rates to drop before refinancing. We managed to get a seven-and-a-half percent rate in the early 90s. This is how we got to Irvine, where we would live for twenty-one years.

Chapter 17 is about how we parented, how it sometimes mattered, and how it sometimes did not.

CHAPTER 17:

What My Wife and I Did That Made Us Good Parents

We gave our children more than a few minutes of our time during their upbringing and could be considered the first "helicopter" parents. Dr. Coleman writes that "Research psychologist Diana Baumrind has influenced many parents and psychologists with her theory of authoritative parenting. It's a useful concept I often suggest to parents looking for general guidelines. From this perspective, there are three types of parents: authoritarian, permissive, and authoritative. Authoritarian parents are characterized by using too much control and showing little affection. Permissive parents are characterized by showing a lot of affection and very little control. Authoritative parents show a lot of affection and a lot of control. Her findings reveal that all things considered, authoritative parents are the best predictor for successful development." (Coleman 11).

My ex-wife and I had an authoritative approach to raising our children. We were not into the authoritarian approach to parenting because we did not want our children to hate us for being too strict. We wanted them to learn to make good choices and be happy. However, since our parents were not good models, my ex-wife and I were not experts in raising children, but we did our best without knowing these three models. We managed to instinctively operate as good parents because we knew what our children did not want to experience. Although we operated as authoritative parents, we also overindulged our parenting to the exclusion of each other, as I have already indicated. Because the two of us came from poor parenting, we worked hard to be better parents than our parents and perhaps went too far to prove that.

First and foremost, we both emphasized the importance of education to the children, and it was understood that they would go to college. We started their education by reading to them. We read tons of books to them and emphasized the importance of reading and enjoying reading. We read to the kids as often as we could. Even after a long day of work (teaching was quite tiring), we would sit down and read to them before they went to sleep. We played with language with them and had toys that helped improve their understanding of letters, numbers, and symbols. They had two educated teachers to help them with their work. We did so throughout their school days, often helping them with a paper late at night to have it ready for submission the next day. We both worked hard to achieve the goals we set for them. They were straight "A" students throughout grammar school and junior high school and received just a few "B's" in high school partly because some teachers were "hard-core." By the time the kids went to college, they were fully prepared for those rigors: one went to Stanford on a golf scholarship, and the other went to the University of California at Santa Barbara.

We also provided them with good memories of holidays and birthdays. During all those years, they had a birthday party at every age through high school. Their Christmas times were replete with goodies in the stockings and presents under the tree. Santa was always good to them. The Easter Bunny provided gifts, trips, money, and candy for a delightful spring. They picked up eggs in the backyard through 6th grade. In short, these were two kids who got it all. There was never anything that they wanted that they did not get. To their credit, they were not demanding children and were happy with the gifts they received.

Regarding sports activities, I was always very involved with the kids. I coached baseball and soccer for several years. I worked with them to improve their skills; they were both excellent athletes. When my son became a good player at golf, I dedicated myself to helping him improve his game. While it is always a tenuous position to be the Dad and the coach, there are problems one can expect. My son needed to perform well to gain the attention of the college coaches. Eventually, that was achieved, and he received a scholarship to Stanford to play golf for the team. The father and the son need a great deal of dedication to achieve that goal. My daughter was an excellent soccer player and made varsity as a freshman in high school at a good athletic school. She was not good enough to play at the college level but loved the game. We practiced her skills in local fields.

When it came to a balanced approach to bringing them up, my ex-wife and I had an authoritative approach to their growing up. The authoritative approach allows for both discipline and affection. It is a balance of both. We were not into the authoritarian approach to parenting because we did not want our children to hate us for being too strict. We did not want them to rebel like most children from authoritarian parenting. We also did not want to be so lax that they could do whatever they pleased. Often, it was challenging to say no to them when they wanted something we did not think was appropriate for the time. We wanted them to learn to make good choices.

Aside from the athletic support we gave the children, we helped them academically. Since I was a high school and college English teacher, I helped them write papers for high school assignments and their college papers. I helped by critiquing their papers and typing them when it was late at night and they had other studying to do. Both excelled in school. Their academic performance was achievable because they were taught to read by the time they were five years old.

Even after graduating high school, I helped them with their college papers. Sometimes, I had to drop everything else to work with the papers they sent me from college. There was never a time that I was not available to help them finish their papers. Once my son had a midnight deadline to submit the paper, I worked on it late to revise it. I was always there to help both of them.

Both were the kind of kids that any parent wants to have. They both liked school and worked hard to achieve good grades. I am sure that anyone raising kids would want them. Yet, it was not always peaches and cream. There were issues that we struggled to overcome. One of those issues was my son's stubbornness. My ex-wife read books about it to learn more about what to do with someone like that. Also, he developed an attention deficit disorder in high school and had to take Adderall. This did not present family problems, but it detracted from his ability to sustain long periods of concentration, so work took much longer than usual. So, he had to be bailed out from time to time.

There certainly wasn't anything we would not do for those kids. I worked a second job to make money to keep a golf country club membership so that my son could develop his skills. I have written another book about his accomplishments. I spent an enormous time working on his game to achieve his dream of getting a golf scholarship at Stanford. I took care of three rental properties, taught part-time at the community college, taught full-time at the high school, sold real estate part-time, and taught golf to country club members. The college teaching earnings were used to support my son's golf. I made a Herculean effort to give my son and daughter a good start in life.

While the kids were growing up, there was harmony 95% of the time. In other words, we did not fight the kids and had a lot of cooperation. There definitely were moments when there were disagreements, but they were quickly resolved, and all was normal again. Since it has been twenty-five years since they graduated from high school, I may need to remember things, but I cannot remember any significant issues we had. We did not confront the kids about drugs because, to our knowledge, they did not partake in them.

The final chapter compares the Parenting Manifesto of Brene Brown to our efforts as parents. This is a measure of how well we conducted ourselves as parents compared to the model that Brene suggests for ideal parenting.

CHAPTER 18:

How Our Parenting Compared to Brene Brown's Wholehearted Parenting Manifesto

B rene Brown, the notable social scientist, declared in her Wholehearted Parenting Manifesto (found in her book *Daring Greatly)* that checking what we did well and failed at as parents is essential. I will write the words of her parenting manifesto and then comment on whether we managed to do what might be considered great parenting. Each of the characteristics of her manifesto is one that parents would ideally practice. The purpose is to show how well my ex-wife and I parented.

Brene Brown: "Above all else, I want you to know you are loved and lovable. You will learn this from my words and actions—the lessons on love are in how I treat you and myself."

There is no question that both of us, as parents, loved our children and that they were both lovable. Our actions and our words were demonstrations of our love for them. We, as parents, succeeded at that. We would do anything for them. A friend's letter at my daughter's wedding was evidence of that. The letter was a beautiful tribute to my daughter from her friend Talia Berman, who indicated what great characteristics my daughter had. We had all of our friends compliment the success of raising the two of our children. We succeeded on this account of the manifesto.

Brene Brown: "I want you to engage with the world from a place of worthiness. You will learn that you are worthy of love, belonging, and joy whenever you see me practice self-compassion and embrace my imperfections."

I am sure we were unaware of this behavior, so teaching one to practice self-compassion was just something over our heads. Not teaching them self-compassion is indicated by the fact that they both lack compassion for the suffering of others. As to accepting their parents' imperfections, they have failed miserably at learning that reality. As parents, we are not perfect. Something was missing in that message.

Brene Brown: "We will practice courage in our family by showing up, letting ourselves be seen, and honoring vulnerability. We will share our stories of struggle and strength. There will always be room in our home for both."

They were learning to be courageous, which means being willing to fail and allowing themselves to be vulnerable, but there was not enough failure and not enough failure to teach them how to deal with it. This should have been practiced more during their upbringing. What generations of people before them managed to learn about addressing the challenges of life is that they learned to fail. Neither of them learned to fail. We did not teach them to be courageous and learn to fail because their generation received trophies when they failed in a baseball game instead of being told they were losers and dealing with it. We did not say "they lost" after the game and taught them what losing means. We did not want to damage their precious egos, instead making the most selfish generation in the history of man. Dr. Coleman comments on this problem: "Coaches of children's sports activities began to give children trophies at the end of the season, regardless of whether they were on the losing or winning team. While parents before the twentieth century believed that the rigors of competition and strain would strengthen their children, contemporary parents began to fear that comparison with other children would leave them feeling insecure, discouraged, or damaged. Parents increasingly worried they weren't doing enough to develop and protect their children's self-esteem." (Coleman 66). Instead of damaging egos, they were inflated to the point of developing a generation of narcissists. I do not doubt that this was a by-product of their upbringing.

Brene Brown: "We will teach you compassion by practicing compassion with ourselves first, then with each other. We will set and respect boundaries and honor hard work, hope, and perseverance. Rest and play will be family values, as well as family practices."

We did not teach them to be compassionate because they demonstrate that they have little compassion for those who are suffering. Whether we failed as parents to get that lesson across through church or our everyday lives is a failing I am sure both of us are sorry for. The most significant evidence was that my son had little regard for my suffering after the car accident. After the accident, I was stuck in the car without the ability to open the door and let myself out. I was screaming for help, and my son was down the street talking to a stranger about the accident. Instead of ensuring his father's safety, he chatted with someone he did not know. Another stranger who saw my distress came to the door, wrenched it open, and took off my seatbelt. Had the car exploded before, I would have died in a burning holocaust. To know compassion, one has to be taught compassion, and Brene Brown believes it is the family's responsibility to do that. I also think that religion will teach one compassion to be empathetic, sympathetic, and compassionate for those suffering. To say that my son and daughter care about the suffering of my wife, who is struggling with two debilitating problems of Trigeminal Neuralgia and Lung Cancer, just demonstrates a complete lack of compassion for other people, especially their own family. I am sure they are both more compassionate toward their dogs than they are toward their immediate family members.

Brene Brown: "You will learn accountability and respect by watching me make mistakes and make amends and by watching how I ask for what I need and talk about how I feel."

On this account, we as parents were failures because the word respect does not exist in their vocabulary, even if the parents earned it. My children also have no interest in making amends for mistakes that people make. They have no tolerance for people who make mistakes, even though they are far from perfect. The whole idea of honoring the mother and the father is out the window with this generation. If they choose not to honor the parent anymore, throwing them under the bus is their solution to the parental problem.

This may be the highlight of our failure as parents. Yet, we did our best, and my daughter's friend's letter tells us we were much more successful as parents than we thought. Those other factors have led them to do what they have done despite our efforts: their family history, their genes, their culture of Millennial narcissists, and other media influences.

Brene Brown: "I want you to know joy so we can practice gratitude together."

Gratitude is not one of my children's virtues. Because they thought their upbringing was "normal," they did not think it was that special, but they failed to realize that both parents came from nothing and had to earn everything on their own while most of what my children needed was provided for them. We did not practice gratitude. We did not teach them to be grateful for what they had. Once, I received a Father's Day card from my daughter and my son thanking me for being a great father. Even though I once was, they hardly believe that now. Cicero said, "Gratitude is the father of all virtues." Sadly, they did not demonstrate that enough in their engagements with me.

Brene Brown: "I want you to feel joy; together, we learn how to be vulnerable."

When someone is susceptible to physical or emotional attack or harm, they are vulnerable. Since Brene became famous for her Ted Talk explaining the need to learn to be vulnerable, this is something that was way beyond our scope as parents, but as parents, we learned vulnerability through our failures. They didn't. They did not learn to fail, so they did not learn to deal with adversity. They could not handle adversity because they were not taught vulnerability through learning how to fail. Their "entitled" generation had far too much success and not enough failure. Brene says that the entitlement cure is practicing gratitude. Something they never did. Something they never learned well enough. Something we never practiced as a family. I am grateful for the things I have in my life and to be alive. I am not grateful for the way my children have treated me. Perhaps it was because they never learned to be genuinely grateful.

Brene Brown: "When uncertainty and scarcity visit, you can draw from the spirit that is a part of our everyday life."

In short, when trouble times come, her children will be prepared because of the practices they have in their family. Fortunately, they never had uncertainty and scarcity because their mother and I worked hard. All that they needed was always there. Our teaching jobs allowed us to keep the ship floating without hesitation in good and bad economic times. Our jobs were steady, and economic downturns did not affect us like others. In a way, that was too bad, for learning to do without is what Brene is talking about. Our courage to keep rental properties as a means to provide for their college education was quite daring because we did not have the means to support empty rentals.

Brene Brown: "Together, we will cry and face fear and grief. I will want to take away your pain, but instead, I will sit with you and teach you how to feel it."

Brene Brown strongly advocates failure, challenging oneself, and seeing how things turn out. We kept them from failure, and our generation brought up kids shielded from pain and failure because we did not want their egos to be damaged. The problem, as a result, was the creation of a massive number of narcissists. Ironically, they think tossing around that word is easy, but the reality is that their generation is the whole of them. People who think about nothing but themselves don't know empathy, compassion, failure, and struggle. We failed miserably on that one.

Brene Brown: "We will laugh and sing and dance and create. We will always have permission to be ourselves with each other. No matter what, you will always belong here."

We did manage to laugh and sing and dance and create. We had a good home environment for them. Christmas music was played the entire season; the Easter Bunny arrived every year with eggs to pick up all around the house, and gifts and presents abounded in our house. It was almost an ideal childhood. We laughed, sang, played, and loved our children as best we could.

Brene Brown: "As you begin your Wholehearted journey, the greatest gift I can give you is to live and love with my whole heart and dare greatly."

Brene challenges her kids to dare greatly and courageously do what is difficult. She expects them to put themselves in the fray, face complex challenges, and learn to fail in the arena of daring greatly. We had yet to learn about setting them up for that kind of challenge, but they managed to get to work right out of college and support themselves. That is success all by itself. They did take on the challenge of college, but how could they fail when they did not have to pay for it, did not have to work outside of school for it, and never had to face the adversity of how the money was going to be there when the bills came due?

Brene Brown: "I will not teach of love or show you anything perfectly, but I will let you see me, and I will always hold sacred the gift of seeing you. Truly, deeply, seeing you."

Neither of our children's parents were perfect and should be accepted as such. They both did not like some of the decisions we made as parents, but we made those decisions in our and their best interests. Again, to repeat an important story, I remember my son wanting to snowboard just before the finals of high school golf in his senior year. He so bugged me about doing that I finally had to say no for good. Since he had never snowboarded before, I could imagine if he had broken a wrist and never participated in the high school championships that year. The Stanford coach told us he would offer him a scholarship at the end of his junior year, but he needed to show how good he was. When he won his second high school championship in the spring of his junior year, the coach thought he would be the next NCAA champion from Stanford. Would the coach have offered that scholarship if my son had not participated and won that championship? That scholarship got him a degree from Stanford and a great job at Google for eighteen years. Despite my insistence on not snowboarding, my son did not like being told no.

Their mother and I were not perfect parents, and no one is. Even the so-called parenting experts make mistakes. We did make mistakes, according to Brene Brown's Parenting Manifesto. Their adult behavior evidences this, but it may also be due to factors beyond the teaching we, as parents, gave them. Instead of abandoning me, my children should be praising me for my efforts as a father, but they did not learn all the lessons of good parenting that Brene Brown suggests; otherwise, they would not be doing what they are doing. The perfect paradigm for the American family is illustrated on the

TV program *Blue Bloods* at the end of each of their shows: The entire family gets together for dinner, all generations are represented, and each shares their triumphs and failures. As a result, every person learns from each other about how to deal with adversity in the problematic world that America is today. We need to move more to being family than separate individuals who are impervious to the feelings of others. It is a lesson they still need to learn.

Chapter 19 shares what I did as a grandparent to endear myself to them. Although I made mistakes, it has cost me a great deal to lose them. None of them were mistakes that could not be remedied. None of them were serious mistakes. At least, I didn't think so.

CHAPTER 19 :

What I Did to Be a Good Grandparent

W hile my son may disagree that I was a good grandparent, the reader should know that I did many things to endear myself to his two children and my daughter's child. When the two children were born, my son and his wife lived in Northern California, and I lived in the San Diego region. I traveled to see them and celebrate their arrival just after birth. Although I was not there at the time of the birth, I believed this was a particular time for the parents and not the right time for the grandparents. This can be debated ad infinitum. I spent time with the family and took pictures of my new grandson and granddaughter. I celebrated their arrival.

Before long, my son and his wife decided to raise the kids in Ireland, where she was born. While they were in Ireland, I made four trips to see them. I made two trips to care for them and walk them to school. These two trips were designed to allow the kids to get to know Grandpa. Both trips were to spend time with the children and have fun with them, and we did. I wanted to do it anyway because I felt that grandparents were important in the grandchildren's lives. My other two trips were visiting them, seeing the country, and playing golf.

When my son and his wife returned to the United States, they took jobs at Google in Boulder, Colorado. My wife and I decided to move there and be closer to their family. We moved from Indio, California, to Colorado, and although we lived in Colorado Springs, it was about an hour and a half drive to Boulder. We joined them on several occasions and had great fun there. During our stay there, we babysat the children several times. We loved being with those two kids. We had a lot of fun with them.

Whenever I got together with the kids, I played Grandpa Monster, which they loved. I played cards with them, took them for ice creams, and taught them golf skills at the driving range, like hitting the golf ball, chipping, and putting. I was as involved with them as I could be. I also read to them and talked to them about their reading. They were both brilliant kids and very curious. We had a good relationship, and I always received cards from them from Ireland during the holidays they made, especially for my wife and me.

I walked to school with both kids for two weeks on two different visits to Ireland. I wanted them to know how much I cared about them. I wanted them to remember me well when they grew older and recalled that Grandpa walked us to school and picked us up after school. While I loved golf a great deal, golfing in Ireland would have been the ideal thing for me to do, but instead, I chose to walk those kids to school and play grandparent to them before and after school until my son and his wife came home from their work at Google at five to five-thirty. We had a wonderful time together.

I played soccer with them in the field near the house, and we played cards in the morning before school. I got them to pack their lunch and disciplined them when necessary. We played a lot of soccer in the afternoon when school was over. I sacrificed my stay with them in Ireland instead of just golfing around the country, which I dearly would have loved to do. I managed to get in some golf on one of the visits, but I was sure to return in time for their exit from the school.

I did all I could to give them presents for their birthdays, Christmas, and other holidays. I loved those kids, and I would assume they loved me, knowing that they would run out the door at their house and come to hug me. But all of those efforts meant nothing to my son and his wife.

When my daughter became pregnant, I went to see her in Seattle to be with her before her daughter was born. When her daughter was born, I went to see her, and on the second occasion, I walked my granddaughter around the block for hours to allow her mother to rest. I visited Seattle to be and stay with their family and enjoy my granddaughter. She was great fun, and every visit was precious time with her.

I always took advantage of every opportunity to send her holiday gifts. I wanted my granddaughter to know that her grandpa loved her. Before she was born, I contributed to a fund to help bring that child into the world, as my daughter had gone through several sessions of in vitro. I say all these things to argue that I did my best as a grandparent all along the way.

Estranging parents and grandparents is behavior that is the beginning of the end of the family in America. I do not say this to be dramatic, but the spiraling down of the family has been happening for a very long time. Since the 1960s, the family has dissipated into a mixed family, and the complete rejection of the importance of extended family has exaggerated that decline. The typical two-parent family has declined dramatically. Older adults are just not necessary. They are expendable. And they are being expended at dramatic rates. The extended family is becoming less and less critical, and the family unit is breaking apart. We see this from the Millennial generation and Generation Z.

The lesson I have learned is that my son and daughter-in-law do not value the teachings of the grandparent to the grandchild. Too many of this generation only give a modest regard for their grandparents. Disregarding older people is the first step in destroying the family unit. This practice will continue to decline the family unit as the next generation sees what this generation has done. I could not even imagine doing something like this to my parents, much less exercising this action. My parents were not perfect, but we never thought of taking them out of our children's lives. There is too much to lose and a great deal to gain. Let that be the final lesson to those readers who think this action is necessary to protect the children from grandparents. I understand that it is necessary if the grandparent is abusive to the grandchildren in any way. Still, I cannot agree with estrangement over the simple mistake of challenging them about an ancestry report.

Conclusion

Finally, Dr. Coleman says, "Many of those who contact me are some of the most dedicated, educated, and loving parents of any generation." I was one of those dedicated and educated parents who loved my children and my grandchildren to the best of my ability but still became an estranged parent and grandparent. The purpose of this book has been to allow estranged parents to realize that they are not responsible for their children's choices to estrange them. I have learned that this is a social phenomenon that has occurred at the expense of the Baby Boomer generation, who hovered over their children to a fault. We Baby Boomers are the original "Helicopter" parents who met our children's every need, protected them unwittingly from failure, did not teach them how to address adversity, and suffered the "slings and arrows of outrageous fortune" for doing so. In part, because they did not learn failure successfully, they did not learn to deal with adversity. Instead, their solution is to eliminate what they perceive to be the problem when they, themselves, are the problem. We are not witches, although we have been deemed such. Society has ostracized us after being deemed a witch, and family has ostracized us for speaking out about being recognized as a grandparent.

The most important lesson learned is that it is not our fault for bringing about estrangement. We are not the ones who have chosen to cut off our contact with our children and grandchildren. It is a choice by adult children, perhaps to "protect" their children. In short, I cannot take responsibility for such behavior since I would never dream of doing such a thing to my mother and father, even though they were less than stellar parents. But this generation is different and has decided to "jangle the keys of the kingdom" and tell the parents they are no longer in control. They are adults who feel it is best to keep Grandpa away from the grandchildren so they do not suffer from his behavior. To all the parents who have suffered the same fate, especially those Dads who are mistreated more so than mothers, take heart in knowing that you are not alone and hopefully find some solace in this reading.

Another lesson learned is that my adult children's children will perpetuate this behavior by one day estranging their parents. The adult children's children will practice the upbringing they learned from their parents. This will ensure that their children will resist them when they become adults. More importantly, the fact that their children have been subjected to the ruthless tearing away of a grandparent will never go away in their minds. Those children will remember when Grandpa "disappeared," and they will learn as adults why that happened, perhaps through reading this book. If the grandparent lives long enough, they can speak to the grandchildren as adults and tell their side of the story.

I learned that my children cannot accept that a parent or a grandparent is imperfect. If my children were perfect, I would willingly accept the criticism of not being worthy of my grandchildren's attention. Instead, their decision to remove a grandparent from their child's life will have long-lasting ramifications that may carry on for several generations and continue to usher in the decline of the American family. Perhaps only time will tell if this comes to fruition, but chances are that it will. I have already shown that when the family history includes the shunning of a parent, it is bound to be repeated. I believe one of the factors in my ousting was due to the history of shunning my ex-wife's family in the previous generation. It has become a part of the current generation and will likely continue for several more. It may be that the reasons for shunning will be even more ridiculous than the current one of objecting to not being recognized as a grandparent in my grandson's fourth-grade ancestry report. Wow, talk about egregious behavior on my part!

Some additional lessons I learned was that despite being wrong, why can't people take responsibility for making an error? Why is it that a generation of individuals believes they are entitled to do whatever they want regardless of the hurt that they cause? More importantly, what does this teach the children when a grandparent is expendable? Why does anyone even think that way?

People may experience the same thing with their children because they have taught them that it is okay to dump the parents in the trash can for almost any reason. Grandchildren will not forget what their parents did, and whatever excuses they gave them will be dispelled when they reach adulthood and figure out that they were cheated out of grandparents who loved them. As we have learned, it is in their genes and their generational behavior because they have reinforced that this is an okay thing to do. They have earned their reputation because the research validates it.

I wake up every morning, and my thoughts go to writing about this problem, and now it is finished. I hope my fellow sufferers feel the pain from what I wrote because that is what I want them to feel. I've had enough of their abuse, so I wrote this to show them how I feel and how it feels to be an abused elder. They should live with the shame of it for the rest of their lives, and their karma is yet to happen. Go ahead and continue to "jangle the keys of the kingdom" because one day, those keys will be in their children's hands.

Afterword

"As a man thinketh in his heart, so is he"

***Book of Proverbs*, chapter 23, verse 7**

I n the "Afterword" of Joshua Coleman's book *When Parents Hurt: Compassionate Strategies When You and Your Grown Child Don't Get Along,* he suggests several essential principles for healing, and one of them is to "develop an identity and life story based on your strengths and achievements as a parent and individual, instead of a story about your suffering or failures." (278). Even though this writing is not exactly what Dr. Coleman wanted, this book did show the effort I made as a father and grandfather for my children and grandchildren; it also tells the story of what was done for my children as they grew up. Although the book discusses the suffering I have endured due to estrangement, it was to share with those estrangers how their estrangement impacts their recipients. Each of those readers who found themselves in similar situations like mine should do the same thing. Indeed, the reader does not have to write a book as I have, but a good exercise would be to list all those positive things each did as a parent and all those positive things each did as a grandparent. Write down the achievements of each, and take pride in what was accomplished.

Dr. Coleman also suggests giving something back to society in his Essential Principles for Healing. This book is my giving back. It is a hopeful message to those parents who have suffered the indignity of estrangement. My message is clear: This is a social phenomenon that we are victims of, and we must not take full responsibility for this happening. Although we fostered the estrangement in some way, we are not alone in carrying out the act of actually doing this. We cannot accept full responsibility for this happening. Our adult children need to take responsibility for this happening and work to solve the crisis we have here in America. If we cannot do so, we will head toward an impending doom to our social structure. The way of the Roman Empire.

Finally, Dr. Coleman relates about support: "And it's through support that we develop compassion to forgive ourselves and others. Through support, we learn we're not alone in our suffering. And it is through support that we are reminded of all that we have, for which to be grateful." (279). I am eternally grateful for his support during this challenging time.

With that, I leave the reader with the words of a famous Portugal Poet, Fernando Pessoa:

"You can have flaws, be anxious, and even be angry, but remember that your life is the world's biggest contest." Only you can stop it from failing. You are appreciated, admired, and loved by so many. Remember that happiness does not have a sky without storms, a road without accidents, a job without effort, or a relationship without disappointments.

"Being happy means finding strength in forgiveness, hope in battles, security in fear, love in discord." It's not only to enjoy the smile but also to reflect on the sadness. It's not just about celebrating success. It's about learning from failure. It's not just about feeling happy with applause; it's about being happy anonymously. Being happy is not a fatality of destiny but an achievement for those who can travel independently.

"Being happy is to stop feeling victimized and become the author of your destiny." "It is to walk through deserts, but to find an oasis deep in one's soul. It's thanking God every morning for the miracle of life. To be happy is not to be afraid of your feelings and to be able to talk about yourself. Have the courage to hear a "no" and trust the criticism, even when it's unwarranted. It's about hugging your kids and parents and spending poetic moments with your friends, even when they hurt us.

"To be happy is to let the creature that lives in us live, free, joyful, and simple." You are mature enough to say, "I made mistakes." Having the courage to say I'm sorry. It's the sense of saying, "I need you". It's having the ability to say, "I love you". May your life become a garden of blissful opportunities that in spring is a lover of joy and in winter a lover of wisdom.

"And when you make a mistake, start over." Because only then will you be in love with life. You will discover that happiness isn't about having a perfect life. But use tears to irrigate the tolerance. Use your defeats to train your patience.

"Use your mistakes with the serenity of the sculptor." Use the pain to connect to pleasure. Use obstacles to open the windows of intelligence. Never give up. Above all, never abandon the people who love you. Never stop being happy because life is a fantastic show."

After two years of being unable to see my grandchildren or speak to them, I wrote this email to my daughter-in-law and told her how I felt. It demonstrates how painful estrangement can be for a grandparent.

M——,

In my life, I never would have imagined being shut out of seeing my grandchildren or even talking to them. From your perspective, there must be a need to keep them out of my life. That is your choice. And I have done what I can to respect that.

I have just one thing to say about it. It has been the most painful experience of my life by far. I cannot tell you how hurtful this has been for me and my wife. This is NOT to make you feel guilty but just to let you know that it is nothing like I have gone through with anything. I lost sleep over it for a year and a half until I met my psychologist. He has helped me cope with the hurt.

For three years after the auto accident, I was in physical pain every night with muscle spasms that hit me in the middle of the night at a 7 to 10 level and made me scream out without being able to control myself. By a miracle, an acupuncturist alleviated my pain after several sessions. I am pleased about that, even though some pain persists. It is not perfect, but I don't scream out anymore.

I say this because all of that physical pain pales compared to the emotional pain of losing a relationship with grandchildren I love so much.

You do not have to do anything about this. I am just telling you what it has been like for me and my wife, who loves those kids as much as I do. Since two years have passed, I assume many more years will pass without their being in our lives. We are resigned to this.

Take care,
Grandpa/Dick

This letter captures the emotional pain of becoming estranged. All I could do was send notes, emails, and phone calls of apology for doing something wrong that was so horrible to them. But I am still awaiting a response even though I gave her an out about responding. Anyone who received such a plea for help would think there would be a response. But I am still waiting for a response. They do not care about the pain I am in.

So I have hope of getting together with them again. It tears my heart every day to be unable to be a part of their lives, and I know many parents out there suffer the same fate. This is what prompted me to write this book. It is for all those suffering the same fate, especially those who were good parents and did not deserve this vial treatment. I am sorry for the trouble I caused, and I cannot apologize any more than I have. This has been my way of putting this behind me for good. My life is limited, and I want to spend it wisely and not be bothered by what I cannot control.

A Final Word

There are so many emotions that one travails when one is estranged, and none are good. I shared those with the estrangers so they might elevate their consciousnesses to realize how painful and damaging such an action is to aging parents and grandparents. I have also tried to share with the estranged how they can improve their situation with more understanding of what is happening to them. Many people cannot grasp the enormity of the mental challenge that being estranged is. Over time I spent reading and exploring to try to understand what I was going through, I came across a Youtube presentation by a psychologist who was suggesting how to heal the conflict. Below the presentation was an opportunity for those who listened to her presentation a chance to respond. One of the comments made caught my attention. Here it is:

@kellyyork3898
1 month ago
I say let them.[she means estrange the parents] It's not a parent's job to keep parenting and watching over kids for the rest of their kid's life. If they hate you, so be it. They don't want to ever see you again? Well, good riddance. Grieve if you have to and go on with your life. Have fun with friends, go on long vacations, cultivate love, adopt a pet, give your money to other needy children and charities. Have a blast with the rest of your life. Life is too short to be wrapped up in this type of constant drama. Surround yourself with

healthy, good people who love you for you. And don't leave your "estranged children" one red cent….even if they show up acting all "lovey dovey" as you lay dying. :)

My wife and I believe Kelly hit the nail on the head. We have adopted a pet and moved on with our lives. This book was "finished" several months ago, and I have delayed publication in the hopes of reconciliation. It does not look like that is going to happen. So, I added this comment to the manuscript before publication in 2024. We have taken Kelly's advice: We have established a lot of friendships, we have gone on vacations, and we have given to people in need. We have surrounded ourselves with healthy, good people who love us for ourselves. Our children are out of the will. Good riddance. We do not want to share time with "toxic" adult children who continue to be children despite reaching adulthood.

Works Cited

INTRODUCTION

Coleman, Joshua. *Rules of Estrangement: Why Adult Children cut Ties and How to Heal the Conflict.* Harmony Books, 2020.

Coleman, Joshua. *When Parents Hurt: Compassionate Strategies When You and Your Grown Child Don't Get Along..* HarperCollins Publishers, 2008.

Miller, Arthur. *The Crucible.* Penguin Classics, 1953.

CHAPTER 1

Chapman, Fern Schumer. January 2, 2023. "Why are So Many Families Living with Estrangement?" 11-7-2023. <https://www.psychologytoday.com/us/blog/brothers>

Coleman, Joshua. *Rules of Estrangement: Why Adult Children cut Ties and How to Heal the Conflict.* Harmony Books, 2020.

DeVise, Daniel. 7-19-2023. "One Quarter of Adult Children Estranged from a Parent." 11-7-2023. <https://thehill.com/blogs/blog>-

Miller, Arthur. *The Crucible.* Penguin Classics, 1953.

CHAPTER 2

Brown, Brene. *Daring Greatly.* April 7, 2015.

CHAPTER 3

Martin, Sharon. July 19, 2023. "The Effects of Estrangement." 11-12-2023 <https://www.livewellwithsharonmartin.com/effects-of-family-estrangement/>

Wildey, Sharon. *Abandoned Parents: The Devil's Dilemma.* 2014.

CHAPTER 4

Brown, Brene. *Daring Greatly: How the Courage to Be Vulnerable Transforms the Way We Live, Love, Parent and Lead.* September 11, 2012

Coleman, Joshua. *When Parents Hurt.* HarperCollins Publishers, 2008.

Ekman, Paul and Goleman, Daniel. *Knowing Our Emotions, Improving Our World.* January 1, 2007.
Harrison, G. B. *The Complete Works of Shakespeare.* January 1, 1952.

Hemingway, Ernest. *A Farewell to Arms.* 1929

Hidayat, Wahyu. "The Influence of Adversity Quotient on Students' Mathematical Understanding Ability." *Journal of Physics*, February 2019.

Norton, Amy. "Adult Children Far More Likely to Be Estranged From Dad Than Mom." *Health Day News*, December 20, 2022.

Roosevelt, Teddy. "Citizenship in a Republic" April 23, 1910. Sorbonne in Paris, France.

The Bible. King James Version, 2010.

CHAPTER 6

Coleman, Joshua. *When Parents Hurt: Compassionate Strategies When You and Your Grown Child Don't Get Along.* HarperCollins Publishers, 2008.

CHAPTER 7

Coleman, Joshua. *When Parents Hurt: Compassionate Strategies When You and Your Grown Child Don't Get Along.* HarperCollins Publishers, 2008.

Coleman, Joshua. Rules of Estrangement: *Why Adult Children Cut Ties and How to Heal The Conflict.* Harmony Books, 2020.

Coleman, Joshua. "How Many Children Have Cut Contact with Their Parents?" *The Economist.* May 20, 2021.

Coleman, Joshua. "A Shift in American Family Values is Fueling Estrangement." *Atlantic Magazine.* January 10, 2021.

CHAPTER 8

Coleman, Joshua. When Parents Hurt. HarperCollins Publishers, 2008.

Martin, Sharon. July 19, 2023. "The Effects of Estrangement." 11-12-2023 <https://www.livewellwithsharonmartin.com/effects-of-family-estrangement/>

CHAPTER 9

Coleman, Joshua. *When Parents Hurt: Compassionate Strategies When You and Your Grown Child Don't Get Along.* HarperCollins Publishers, 2008.

CHAPTER 10

Brailovskaia, Julia and Bierhoff, Hans-Werner. "The Narcissistic Millennial Generation: A Study of Personality Traits and Online Behavior on Facebook." *The Journal of Adult Development*. November 23, 2018.

Coleman, Joshua. *When Parents Hurt: Compassionate Strategies When You and Your Grown Child Don't Get Along.*. HarperCollins Publishers, 2008.

Mosias-Sinay, Claudia. "Systemic Narcissism." Medium.com, August 29, 2023. <https://narc-disruptor.medium.com/what-is-systemic-narcissism->

Stein, Joel. "The Me Me Me Generation." *Time Magazine*. May 20, 2013.

CHAPTER 11

Coleman, Joshua. *When Parents Hurt: Compassionate Strategies When You and Your Grown Child Don't Get Along.*. HarperCollins Publishers, 2008.

Coleman, Joshua. Rules of Estrangement: *Why Adult Children Cut Ties and How to Heal The Conflict.* Harmony Books, 2020.

Harrison, G. B. *The Complete Works of Shakespeare*. January 1, 1952.

Hawthorne, Nathaniel. *The Scarlet Letter*. 1850.
Lee, Harper. *To Kill a Mockingbird*. 1960.

CHAPTER 12

Brown, Brene. *Daring Greatly.* Penguin Publishing Group, 2012.

Coleman, Joshua. "A Shift in American Values is Fueling Estrangement." *Atlantic Magazine*, January 10, 2021.

CHAPTER 13

Gilbertson, Tina. "Reconnecting with Your Estranged Adult Child." Psychol-ogytoday.com. November 17, 2018.

CHAPTER 14
Coleman, Joshua. *When Parents Hurt: Compassionate Strategies When You and Your Grown Child Don't Get Along*. HarperCollins Publishers, 2008.

Gilbertson, Tina. "Reconnecting with Your Estranged Adult Child." Psychol-ogytoday.com. November 17, 2018.

CHAPTER 17

Coleman, Joshua. *When Parents Hurt: Compassionate Strategies When You and Your Grown Child Don't Get Along*. HarperCollins Publishers, 2008.

CHAPTER 18

Brown, Brene. *Daring Greatly.* Penguin Publishing Group, 2012.

CONCLUSION

Coleman, Joshua. *When Parents Hurt: Compassionate Strategies When You and Your Grown Child Don't Get Along*. HarperCollins Publishers, 2008.

AFTERWORD
Coleman, Joshua. *When Parents Hurt: Compassionate Strategies When You and Your Grown Child Don't Get Along*. HarperCollins Publishers, 2008.

Acknowledgments

I want to thank my wife, Tina, for persevering in writing this book with me. She has been tireless in her feedback on the writing, and I want to say how much I love her for that.

I want to thank the people at Palmetto Publishing for their outstanding work on this book.

I also want to thank Sue Krenwinkle for her insightful comments about this book. I will use part of her commentary on the cover of my book. Thank you for your kind comments.

And I wish to thank my dear cousin, Claudia Sinay-Mosias, who taught me the difference between venting in a journal and writing a book. Thank you for letting me know the difference between the two.